Where have we come from, and where are we going? In this day and age for China, I am always reminding myself to maintain this sense of history.

– Xi Jinping

From Xi's speech when meeting with foreign attendees of the Second Understanding China Conference in Beijing, *People's Daily*, January 5, 2016

UNDERSTANDING CHINA

"Understanding China" Series

UNDERSTANDING CHINA

ECONOMIC GLOBALIZATION AND CHINA'S FUTURE

Zheng Bijian

CIPG | China International Publishing Group 中国国际出版集团

FOREIGN LANGUAGES PRESS

First Edition 2018

ISBN 978-7-119-11419-4

Published by Foreign Languages Press Co. Ltd
24 Baiwanzhuang Road, Beijing 100037, China
Distributed by China International Book Trading Corporation
35 Chegongzhuang Xilu, Beijing 100044, China
P.O. Box 399, Beijing, China

Printed in the People's Republic of China

PREFACE TO THE "UNDERSTANDING CHINA" SERIES

Zheng Bijian

This series of books covers the topic: Understanding China.

But why is "Understanding China" an important question?

At present, the world around us is going through unprecedented changes and nowhere more so is that the case than in China.

Since the founding of the People's Republic of China in the mid-20th century, and particularly over the past 40 years, a poor and backward country in East Asia with a population of over 1.3 billion has achieved incredible growth to become the world's second largest economy.

It is therefore natural that people should ask: What exactly is going on in China, and what is the secret behind such rapid development?

It is also entirely natural for people to wonder: How can a rising China get along with the rest of the world?

As a result, misgivings about the country abound. All kinds of theories such as the "China threat", the "Collapsing of China", the "Thucydides's Trap" and the "middle income trap" have been directed toward China.

There is no doubt that China should unflinchingly follow its own path and deal with its own matters well. That in itself means that in order to respond to people's concerns, questions and misgivings, one thing must be done – Understand China.

It was precisely for this reason that the China Institute for Innovation & Development Strategy (CIIDS), which I co-founded, joined together with the Chinese People's Institute of Foreign Affairs (CPIFA) and the world-renowned 21st Century Council think tank to hold two Understanding China conferences in 2013 and 2015.

These two important international meetings received the close attention and support of the General Secretary of the CPC and President of China, Xi Jinping, who personally attended and held informal discussions with distinguished overseas participants; and Premier of the State Council Li Keqiang and Vice Premier Zhang Gaoli, who gave the opening speeches at the first and second conferences respectively. Top leaders of departments in the Central Committee of the CPC and State Council also participated alongside senior political figures, experts and scholars from all over the world to undertake face-to-face meetings and answer questions.

The main lesson from the conferences was that confronting questions head-on, being sincere, seeking the truth from facts, and telling the stories of China, the CPC and China's relations with the world, in lively and detailed ways, greatly helps those who care about China to gain new knowledge, and gradually allays the misgivings of those who are uncertain about China.

To achieve this goal we are moving the "Understanding China" international conference to books, videos and online, in order to respond to people's concerns, questions and misgivings on a bigger scale and in more lively forms.

This series has not only received the enthusiastic support of relevant government departments, China International Publishing Group and the Foreign Languages Press, but also the full backing of experienced practitioners, experts and scholars, as well as government leaders.

This is the first set of books in the series. Whilst these are concerned mainly with the works of Chinese writers, future books will also feature writers from other countries.

This is also not simply a collection of books – it will be accompanied by television specials and online videos for people to enjoy.

In our opinion, "Understanding China", including "Understanding the CPC" and "Understanding China's Relations with the World" are all grand undertakings.

Let us passionately follow and participate in these undertakings together.

March 2018

CONTENTS

November 1, 2013. Welcome banquet after the opening ceremony of the First Understanding China Conference

November 2, 2013. At the First Understanding China Conference

November 1, 2015. Opening ceremony of the Second Understanding China Conference

November 1, 2015. Addressing the guests at the welcome banquet after the opening ceremony of the Second Understanding China Conference

Foreword

What has happened to the world and how should we respond? The world, as we know, is changing at a pace and scale that has not been seen in a century. The often bewildering transformation poses a great challenge, not only to the world, but also to the rapidly-developing nation of China. At such times, having the capacity to keep abreast of changing trends and having the courage to lead society forward despite the difficulties is precisely what the glorious tradition of the Communist Party of China (CPC) consists of. During the recently convened 19th CPC National Congress, President Xi Jinping, who is also General Secretary of the CPC Central Committee and Chairman of the Central Military Commission, analyzed the challenges and opportunities in the world today and proposed new and greater contributions for China to make to the human race. He also stated that we must intensify theoretical research and development, and quicken our pace to develop philosophy and social sciences with Chinese characteristics. We, as theoreticians of the Party, have a bounden duty in this regard. Based on my years of research, I think one of the theoretical and strategical imperatives now is to keep in mind the overall situation at home and abroad, follow the guidelines based on Xi Jinping Thought on Socialism with Chinese Characteristics for a New Era, carry out in-depth research on the trend of economic globalization and China's peaceful development road, and on this basis, develop our own theories on development and international relations.

1. Symposium on Philosophy and Social Sciences

On the morning of May 17, 2016, I attended the Symposium on Philosophy and Social Sciences during which President Xi Jinping delivered an important speech.

After the 18th National Congress, in an effort to improve work on publicity, political philosophy, culture, and theoretical research, the Central Committee of the CPC held a series of national conferences on such themes as publicity and political philosophy, art and culture, media communication, cybersecurity and IT applications. President Xi gave important speeches at each of these events. He stated that these conferences were designed as an important vehicle of communication and people could come together to analyze trends, communicate their ideas, build consensus, and plan for China's future. Highly prestigious experts attended the Symposium on Philosophy and Social Sciences. The attendees also included academic leaders with many significant achievements, as well as prominent rising stars, such as consultants or chief experts for the Central Committee project to study and develop Marxist theory, representatives from prestigious national think tanks, students of all levels from institutions of higher education, and senior officials from related agencies. As far as I am able to recall, it is the first time such a high-level symposium has taken place in the field of philosophy and social sciences since the beginning of the reform and opening up. I attended as a seasoned expert and a consultant for the Central Committee project on Marxist theory.

We are aware that philosophy and social science are important tools by which people understand and change the world, and they are a driving power behind historical development and social progress. The degree to which these sciences has evolved in a certain society reflects the capacity of that society to think, its spirit and character, and its level of civilization, and it is also an embodiment of a nation's comprehensive national power and international competitiveness. President Xi has always placed great emphasis on philosophy and social sciences. He has on numerous occasions led the Political Bureau of the CPC Central Committee in studying such social sciences as philosophy, economics, and law, and has also held related conferences so as to drive development in philosophy and social science at the national level. This is very clearly both an ideal in his governance and part of the actualization of the Chinese Dream (the rejuvenation of the Chinese nation).

President Xi's speech was quite efficacious. He emphasized that one must maintain a broad view in observing the current state of China's philosophy and social science, and one must do so within the context of the historical development of China and the world. He stated that every great leap of progress in human society and every great development in human civilization has been closely related to knowledge transformation and pioneering thought in philosophy and social science. The long history of the Chinese civilization has seen a number of philosophies flourish at different time periods, from the pre-Qin Dynasty Hundred Schools of Thought, the study of Confucianism during the two Han dynasties, the metaphysics of the Wei and Jin dynasties, the Buddhism of the Sui and Tang dynasties, the confluence of Buddhism, Confucianism, and Taoism, and the Neo-Confucianism of the Song and Ming dynasties. Since the beginning of Chinese civilization, the Chinese people have produced such schools of thought as Confucianism, Buddhism, Taoism, Mohism, Logicians, Legalism, the Yin and Yang School, Agriculturalism, and Militarism. Some of China's great philosophers include Laozi (dates of birth and death unknown), Confucius (551-479 BC), Zhuangzi (369-286 BC),

Mencius (c. 372-289 BC), Xunzi (c. 313-238 BC), Han Feizi (c. 280-233 BC), Dong Zhongshu (179-104 BC), Wang Chong (27-c. 97), He Yan (?-249), Wang Bi (226-249), Han Yu (768-824), Zhou Dunyi (1017-1073), Cheng Hao (1032-1085), Cheng Yi (1033-1107), Zhu Xi (1130-1200), Lu Jiuyuan (1139-1193), Wang Shouren (1472-1529), Li Zhi (1527-1602), Huang Zongxi (1610-1695), Gu Yanwu (1613-1682), Wang Fuzhi (1619-1692), Kang Youwei (1858-1927), Liang Qichao (1873-1929), Sun Yat-sen (1866-1925), and Lu Xun (1881-1936), all of whom contributed to a great array of cultural heritage. The vast number of great works from ancient China includes an abundance of content on philosophy, social science, and wisdom in governance. These writings were an important basis for people of ancient times to understand and improve the world. They were also important for the whole of Chinese civilization and have been a great contribution to human civilization in general. When President Xi emphasized that "a nation that is underdeveloped in the natural sciences cannot possibly rise to the global forefront, and the same is true for a nation that does not flourish in the realms of philosophy and social science," every expert at the venue felt the burden of their mission for the times and their responsibility to history.

It was at this symposium that President Xi made the earnest proposal of accelerating the speed at which philosophy and social sciences with Chinese characteristics are being built up. He stressed that the features, style, and bearing of philosophy and social science reflect a certain degree of development, a mark of maturity, a symbol of power, and an embodiment of self-confidence. China is a great nation in the fields of philosophy and social science: In terms of research teams, the number of studies written, and government involvement, China ranks among the top in the world. However, academic propositions, thought, viewpoints, standards, and discourse have not yet reached the level or capacity of the nation's comprehensive national power or international position. We must be rooted in China, learn from other countries, research history, seize the day, keep humanity in mind, and move toward the future. We must devote ourselves to developing philosophy and social sciences with Chinese characteristics. We must fully embody China's unique features, style, and bearing in the aspects of the orientation of our thought, our academic system, and our discourse system.

Having said that, what makes up the features of philosophy and social sciences with Chinese characteristics? President Xi believes that they must reflect Chinese tradition and legacy, and at the same time show originality and a readiness to respond to the call of our times. In addition, they must embody systematization and expertise. Indeed, developing philosophy and social sciences with Chinese characteristics requires the integration of resources from the past and present, from China and abroad, and gaining a firm grasp of resources on Marxism, resources on the fine traditional Chinese culture, and resources on philosophy and social science from abroad is of particular importance. That is, we must not forget the past, and as we adopt ideas from abroad, we direct ourselves toward the future. We must look inside, making an in-depth study of the immense subject of people's lives, and we must look outward, actively exploring the massive issue of humanity's prospects and destiny. We must look forward, making accurate assessments of the developmental trends of socialism with Chinese characteristics, and we must look back, carrying forward the fine traditional Chinese culture.

I deeply felt that President Xi's speech was correct in its orientation, directed at the problems of our times and full of detailed facts. It was indeed an insightful guide in our effort to accelerate the speed at which China's unique philosophy and social science are being built up. Moreover, based on current conditions, it is indeed time for developing China's unique socialist philosophy and social sciences.

2. Building up philosophy and social sciences with Chinese characteristics with a focus on the questions of "where from" and "where to"

At the end of the symposium, President Xi asked me, "What have you been working on these days?" I answered, "While you were meeting with political leaders and experts from foreign countries during the 2nd Understanding China Conference[1], you mentioned that the conference was a good platform from which to introduce China to the world. You also stated, 'Where have we come from, and where are we going? In this day and age for China, I am always reminding myself to maintain this sense of history.' I felt that what you said was extremely important, and I began bringing experts in various fields together to write a book series on understanding China. I also plan to make a related film for TV so as

[1] The Understanding China Conference was jointly organized by the China Institute for Innovation and Development Strategy (CIIDS), the Chinese People's Institute of Foreign Affairs, and the world-renowned think tank 21st Century Council. The first (2013) and second (2015) conferences were held in Beijing, each conference drawing over 40 political leaders from foreign countries. The international attendees, Chinese government officials, high-ranking officers of the PLA, and entrepreneurs and experts from China and abroad engaged in sincere and in-depth discussions on the topic of "Understanding China" based on the following: the new global structure, social media and its regulation, whether the Chinese economy can continue to thrive, China's national defense policies, China's decision-making processes, the worldview and international responsibility of the Chinese people, and how to establish an all-inclusive community of common interests. CPC General Secretary Xi Jinping attended both conferences and spoke candidly with international participants. He believes that a conference based on understanding China helps further mutual understanding between China and other countries. The Chinese people are currently working diligently toward realizing the Two Centenary Goals and the Chinese Dream (the rejuvenation of the Chinese nation). The Chinese Dream is linked to the Chinese people's pursuit of good lives as well as the global pursuit of peace and development. In order to fulfill the Chinese Dream, we must persist in upholding socialism with Chinese characteristics, which is the correct path as found by the Chinese people's long and arduous journey of exploration. Premier Li Keqiang and Vice Premier Zhang Gaoli, both of whom are members of the Standing Committee of the Political Bureau of the CPC Central Committee, respectively attended and gave speeches at the openings of the First and Second Understanding China Conferences.

to further introduce China to the world." He was pleased with this response.

The reason I am emphasizing President Xi's question of "Where have we come from, and where are we going?" in the introduction of this book is because I believe it is the central theme of understanding China. Is it not? That is, if we can clearly express where we (as a nation) have come from and where we are going, then have we not come to understand China? I ask the reader to refer to how President Xi discussed this topic with world political leaders and experts during the 2nd Understanding China Conference (November 2015). He stated, "There is a relief sculpture on the Monument to the People's Heroes at Tiananmen Square that depicts China's numerous victories attained from the 1840 Opium War to the success of the Chinese revolution in 1949. ... We cherish the memories of martyrs of the past, and we follow in their steps in pressing forward. We have the Chinese Dream, and we hold the rejuvenation of the Chinese nation as our common denominator."[2] After that, he elaborated on the CPC Central Committee's current policies in answering questions posed by the international participants. That is indeed the state of things: The integration of the tasks China is faced with today with problems of the past is what is necessary to truly and clearly relate China's current strategy for development and policy measures. In fact, President Xi did not only bring up the question of "Where have we come from and where are we going?" just one time. At a forum with instructors and students on core values of socialism at Peking University on May 4, 2015, he said, "A nation, or people of a country, must know who they are, where they came from and where they are heading. Keep on going when you have made your choice."[3]

Everyone knows these three questions originally posed by philoso-

---

[2] *People's Daily*, January 5, 2016.

[3] Xi Jinping: "Young People Should Practice the Core Socialist Values," *Xi Jinping: The Governance of China*, Vol. I, second edition, Foreign Languages Press, 2018, p. 191.

phers of the past: Who am I? Where did I come from? Where am I going? Philosophers have long been exploring the origins of the universe, life, and the human race. Regarding the origin of the latter, the three questions mentioned above are asked. Numerous philosophers have gone through long-term explorations on this question from a diversity of angles and have come up with a number of assumptions related to this ontological question. President Xi, a statesman, has proposed the study of the ontological question of Chinese politics, which of course is also extremely important and could be said to be an even more profound question. In his discussion with professors and students from Peking University, he spoke on the need to promote the core socialist values. He did not, however, speak about values based on values; he instead came from the angle of those foundational three questions in expounding that we are the Chinese people, that Chinese people have the cultural genes of the Chinese ethnicity (which unconsciously influences our thinking and behavior), and that we must carry on the fine traditional Chinese culture. He also stressed that every era has its respective spirit and values. Based on the demands of the era we live in, we must advocate the values of prosperity, democracy, civility, and harmony at the national level, the values of freedom, equality, justice, and rule of law at the social level, and the values of patriotism, dedication, integrity, and friendship at the individual level. Doing so is an embodiment of the demands of socialism, and it allows for the propagation of the fine traditional Chinese culture, allows us to learn from the achievements of other civilizations, and reflects the spirit of the times. This speech should inspire us to study issues such as the core socialist values, China's unique socialist philosophy and social science while keeping at the forefront of our minds the foundational questions of "Who am I?" "Where am I from?" and "Where am I going?" Only by doing this can we make China's unique philosophy and social science reflect Chinese tradition and legacy, and at the same time show originality and a readiness to respond to the call of our times.

This reminds me of another critical issue: Understanding China requires an understanding of the CPC. Only by understanding the latter can one truly understand the China of today. As President Xi Jinping pointed out, "The defining feature of socialism with Chinese characteristics is the leadership of the Communist Party of China." Furthermore, both issues require a solid grasp of the three questions of "Who am I?" "Where am I from?" and "Where am I going?" During the 95th anniversary celebration of the founding of the CPC, President Xi stated that we must remain true to our original aspiration and must forge ahead boldly. During the 19th CPC National Congress, he again stated that we must remain true to our original aspiration and keep our mission firmly in mind. Remain true to our original aspiration means remembering clearly who we are and where we are from; forging ahead boldly and keeping our mission firmly in mind means (on the foundation of understanding who we are and where we are from) to go further and become clear on where we are going. In brief, the three questions are central to our efforts toward the goal of developing philosophy and social sciences with Chinese characteristics as proposed by President Xi.

This theme needs to be firmly grasped in relation not only to domestic issues but also to international issues. For example, President Xi gave a keynote speech entitled "Towards a Community of Shared Future for Mankind" at the UN headquarters in Geneva on January 18, 2017. The speech attracted global attention and had a strong impact. He opened by saying, "...that today's world is full of uncertainties and that people long for a bright future but are bewildered about what lies ahead. What has happened to the world and how should we respond? The world is reflecting on these questions, and they are also very much on my mind. I believe that to answer these questions, we need to be clear about fundamental issues: Where did we come from? Where are we now? And where are we going?"[4] As can be seen, he attributed a vast and complex international issue to those three fundamental questions. He looked back on over 100 years of history, at hot wars and the Cold War, and issues that came up after the Cold War; he stated that the universe only has one earth and that we must cherish it. From there, he proposed the Chinese idea for solving these problems: "The Chinese proposition is: build a global community of shared future and achieve shared and win-win development." His important speech and discussion of problems show us that whether we are studying domestic or international issues, where we are from and where we are going are principal issues.

3. Pride in the peaceful rise of China

In discussing developing philosophy and social sciences with Chinese characteristics, some people have asked whether I was the one who proposed the concept of "the path of China's peaceful rise." I have never shied away from this. It is true, and denying the truth is meaningless. What needs to be pointed out is that the peaceful rise of China and the path of China's peaceful rise are objective facts based on the great changes of the times, and I am only emphasizing this fact. In addition, I am very proud of China's peaceful rise and the associated path it has taken, because I am Chinese.

My ancestral home is in Sichuan of southwestern China. I remember my father said that when my ancestors lived there in 1900, far from Beijing, they heard that the Eight-Nation Alliance had occupied Beijing. When that happened, all the elderly people in his hometown held their

[4] Xi Jinping: "Towards a Community of Shared Future for Mankind," *Xi Jinping: The Governance of China*, Vol. II, Foreign Languages Press, 2017, p. 588

heads and cried. An intense sorrow resulting from national humiliation became rooted deep within the hearts of many Chinese people. Generation after generation of our people have dreamed of the rise of China and held steadfast in pursuing the rejuvenation of the Chinese nation. Beginning with the Opium War, the Chinese people fought for this for 109 years, engaging in bitter struggles until the establishment of the People's Republic of China. Then, during the 1980s, the world entered a period of focus on peace and development, and China's development accelerated with reform and opening up. Such dream and such pursuit are actualized step by step. China is indeed peacefully attaining the rejuvenation of its people along with strength and prosperity for the nation. This is quite an inspiring turn of events for history!

Particularly inspiring is that I have lived through the greatest turnaround since the Third Plenary Session of the 11th Central Committee of the CPC. I personally heard the insight of Deng Xiaoping, the chief architect of reform and opening up, regarding persisting in and developing socialism with Chinese characteristics. I deeply understood that if Deng had held to old ideas and ignored the fact that peace and development were the theme of the times, we might have once again missed the opportunity for the rejuvenation of our nation and our peaceful rise. Deng's proposal that peaceful development was a theme of the times took place over 30 years ago. History has proven that his assessment changed China and is still valid today. For me, his assessment is the basic prerequisite for the ideas of the rise of China and the path of China's peaceful rise.

As workers in China's field of philosophy and social science, there is no reason why we should not study how China has realized such a transformation and such historic progress. There is no reason why we should not place great importance in the Chinese experience created under Deng's leadership and, in turn, refining Chinese theory, which has led to the formation of philosophy and social science with Chinese characteristics. That is to say, in the face of China's peaceful rise, we have an inevitable responsibility to history to research the origins of, conditions for, and challenges faced on the path of China's peaceful rise.

Looking back on history, there is no doubt that the establishment of the People's Republic of China and its socialist system drove the political rise of China, which in turn opened the door to all of China's future progress. The historical event of China's peaceful rise occurred mainly after the reform and opening up. The reform and opening up was a great practice, providing the most solid foundations and prerequisite from which to propel our theories and innovation while creating and allowing for the development of philosophy and social science with Chinese characteristics. All we have done and all of the scientific achievements we have attained can be traced back to that era, to the leadership of the CPC, and to the sinicization of Marxism as advocated by the CPC.

With peace and development being the theme of the times, a huge step forward has been China's reform of establishing a socialist market economy system. Another big step has been linking China to economic globalization (as marked by its entry into the WTO) instead of economic separatism. During the first ten years after entering the WTO, China's national economy saw average annual growth of 10.6%, which also means the overall GDP saw rapid growth. Thus, the eight industrialized nations (except for the US and the Austro-Hungarian Empire, the latter long since having ceased to exist) that had occupied Beijing in 1900 have one-by-one been surpassed economically by China. Russia was the first to be overtaken. Later, between 2000 and 2002, China's GDP surpassed that of Italy and ranked sixth in the world; in 2005, it moved up to fifth place over France; in 2006, it moved up to fourth place over the UK; in 2007, it moved up to third place over Germany; and in 2010, it moved up to second place over Japan (Japan had reached second place in 1968 when it surpassed West Germany). This history of China's economy surpassing that of other countries is part of the story of China's peaceful rise. It is this important fact of history that inspired me to form the following basic concept: With peace and development being the theme of the times, China has independently built up socialism with Chinese characteristics during the process of becoming linked to economic globalization instead of economic separatism. This is my summary of the whole and highly meaningful history of the modernization of Chinese society.

Special gratitude must be given to Deng Xiaoping, the chief architect of the reform and opening up, for the progress made along the path of China's peaceful rise and the resulting benefits for the Chinese people. It is he who led the whole Party in liberating thinking, bringing order from chaos in transferring the focus to economic modernization. It is he who opened the road to socialism with Chinese characteristics, formulating the basic route of "one central task and two basic points." It is he who assessed that the theme of the times was changing from one of war and revolution to one of peace and development. It is he who pointed out that the rapid changes and revolutions in new technology are the perfect opportunities for China to achieve modernization. It is he who made opening up to the world a fundamental policy. It is he who introduced a peaceful foreign policy of independence and autonomy, establishing China's general framework for peaceful and multilateral relations with large nations, neighboring nations, and developing nations. It is he who proposed that China cannot draw lines in foreign affairs based on ideology or social systems, but that we must find common interests with other countries.[5] It is he who emphasized that a socialism with Chinese characteristics is a socialism that helps to constantly develop the productive forces and that favors peace.[6] When all is said and done, Deng Xiaoping Theory is what has made possible the opening up of a path for the peaceful rise of China and the guidance provided by the theoretical system of socialism with Chinese characteristics, which includes Theory of the Three Represents, the Scientific Outlook on Development, and Xi Jinping Thought on Socialism with Chinese Characteristics for a New Era.

[5] While meeting with Henry Kissinger on November 10, 1989, Deng Xiaoping stated, "The era in which the relations between two countries was decided by their social systems has passed. Nations with different social systems can coexist in peace, develop their friendships, and find common interests. China and the US are certainly able to find common interests." *Chronicles of Deng Xiaoping (1975-1997)*, Vol. II, Central Party Literature Press, 2004, Chinese edition, p. 1297.
[6] Deng Xiaoping: "No One Can Shake Socialist China," *Selected Works of Deng Xiaoping*, Vol. III, Foreign Languages Press, 1995, p. 318.

Chapter 1

The Issues and How My Thoughts Have Evolved

As a long-term observer of issues in China and abroad, the main focus of my research is the development of socialism with Chinese characteristics within the context of economic globalization. For a long time, I have maintained a focus on the direction and future of economic globalization, its significance to China, and the strategies China should adopt in response to it.

1. Changes in the underlying trends of the times as the foundation and premise of my thoughts

Those familiar with Chinese politics know that the CPC is China's core leadership in reform and development. According to the Constitution of the CPC, the Party agencies of highest authority are the National Congress and the Central Committee (members of the latter being selected by the former). Thus, every time a National Congress or Central Committee convenes, decisions must be made on reform and development. Furthermore, we know that in China, a great amount of theoretical research (especially on policy) usually occurs around the time that the National Congress and Central Committee convene. Here, I relate how my thoughts on economic globalization and the peaceful rise of China have evolved on a timeline centered on National Congresses.

We must begin with the time period between October of 1987 (13th CPC National Congress) and October of 1992 (14th CPC National Congress). At that time, I was working at the then China Center for International Affairs under the State Council and the Chinese Academy of Social Sciences. Before that, I had worked at the Research Office of Secretariat of the CPC Central Committee. The first time I came across the issue at hand was in April of 1988, and I spoke on it at an international forum: "The world has embarked upon a period of massive transition symbolized by a wave of reform and adjustment on the global scale." The reason for this is that multipolarity had begun to emerge globally and could not be stopped, and the overall structure of the world as established after World War II would be difficult to maintain. Pressed by a series of major imbalances in the global economy, the social systems and economic structures of various countries would also be difficult to maintain. The revolution of new technology was only beginning to unfold, and it was posing nations greater challenges than they had ever faced. Thus, I believed that this would "bring about yet another great transition to the overall structure of world strategies that were established after World War II, and such transition is to be related to the future of the world and every nation during the 21st century."[1] Furthermore, I believed contemporary China was also experiencing a huge, unprecedented social transition. Later, I stated in an essay entitled "Massive Transformation, Becoming Reacquainted," "China, a nation of one billion people that has fallen behind economically and culturally, must achieve national rejuvenation while carrying out modernization and comprehensive reform in the face of developments taking place at the end of the 20th century and the first part of the 21st century. This is a social transition based on socialism that China has never seen before."[2] I also proposed this: "As for speaking of the times, Deng Xiaoping once pointedly stated that peace and development are two great themes for the world of today. He also stated that the global 'East-West issue' is one of peace, and the 'North-South issue' is one of development. This is extremely important for us in scientifically understanding these times."[3] In fact, for all aspects of the wave of reform and adjustment on the global scale mentioned above, the basic premise lies in the fact that the theme of the times, as Deng pointed out, has already transitioned into one of peace and development. This could be said to have been the starting point of the next 30 years of my research work.

---

[1] Zheng Bijian: "Reform and adjustment – sensible choices for the 21st century world," *Essays by Zheng Bijian*, Vol. 1, Shanghai People's Publishing House, 2005, Chinese edition, p. 78.

[2] Zheng Bijian: "Raise the level of understanding of the big changes – deeper and broader researches on theory of primary stage of Chinese socialism," *Essays by Zheng Bijian*, Vol. 1, Shanghai People's Publishing House, 2005, Chinese edition, p. 87.

[3] *Ibid.*, p. 91.

On August 7, 1988, I systematically discussed "the current rise in the wave of reform and adjustment on the global scale" in a published article. Despite not mentioning the term "globalization" at the time, what I had written about was indeed economic globalization. I stated that there were five major factual foundations for this rising wave: The first was that the US and the Soviet Union acknowledged that adverse economic difficulties resulted from long-term military buildups and that the focus of their competition would turn from the military to comprehensive national power, especially in the areas of economy and technology. Second was the strategies that the US was currently debating, such as reforms and adjustments to the structures of the economy, industry, and companies in the US and Western countries, as well as reforms in such areas as administration, taxes, and government spending so as to eliminate "administrative barriers" that hindered market operation and economic development. Third was the new trend toward integration and the G7, symbolizing a major shift and reconfiguration in authority regarding the world economy, and also symbolizing that capitalism was breaking past the limits set by the economic reforms carried out by nations, all of which were developing toward enhancing international cooperation. The fourth was that the Soviet Union and most other socialist countries in Eastern Europe were working hard to propel economic, political, and social reforms and overcome rigidity. The fifth was that developing countries (some including newly industrialized countries) and a large number of low-income countries/regions carried out different reforms and adjustments based on their own specific needs, and a race to gain freedom from poverty through economic and social development was thus initiated. In particular, I pointed out that "a large number of facts show that in many important respects, the reforms and adjustments made in countries with different social systems and at different levels of development, in fact, had many things in common, which could and should allow them to put aside their minor differences to seek common ground."[4] One of these areas of common ground was the emergence of a better-developed "cross-national economy" in the fields of national industrialization, modernization, and the commercialization and socialization of production. It is thus clear that the new "great transition" in the global economy and politics of that time was what later became known as "globalization." Moreover, I stated that countries with different social systems and at different levels of development trending toward international cooperation did not mean the end of conflicts or competition; rather, it was the beginning of a "great race" (or "great war") for comprehensive national power.

I pointed out that reform had already been going on in China for ten years, coinciding nicely with the new wave of reform and adjustment taking place on the global scale, and that China was thus an important component to this global wave. Regarding the outlook for this new trend, I believed it was the peace and development spoken of by Deng Xiaoping. I also stated this was "a great, historical trend on our winding path of existence."[5]

In fact, before the 13th CPC National Congress and during the related preparation and drafting work, I carried out a systematic investigation and work assigned by the CPC Central Committee on the issues of the primary stage of Chinese socialism and socialist market economies. While working on these items, I personally felt the Central Committee's insistence holding to Deng Xiaoping's assessment of peace and development as the theme of the times in handling major international issues and in seizing the opportunity to bring the economies of China and the

---

[4] Zheng Bijian: "On the wave of reform and adjustment on the global scale and on how science and culture are crucial factors for the Great Rejuvenation of the Chinese People," *Essays by Zheng Bijian*, Vol. 1, Shanghai People's Publishing House, 2005, Chinese edition, p. 108.

[5] *Ibid.*, p. 112

world closer together on the foundation of concepts regarding the primary stage of Chinese socialism and socialist market economy. By doing so, China's economic development was greatly promoted. As a theoretician for the CPC, I was very excited, and it further cemented my understanding of China's relationship with the international community.

After the 14th CPC National Congress in 1992, I held the position of executive deputy head of the Publicity Department of the CPC Central Committee, and my main task was to equip the whole Party with Deng Xiaoping's theory on socialism with Chinese characteristics. In September of 1997 before the 15th National Congress, I was made executive vice president of the School of the Central Committee of the CPC (the Central Party School). During the 15th National Congress, Deng Xiaoping Theory was linked to Marxism-Leninism and Mao Zedong Thought as a guiding principle of the Party, and it was written into the Party Constitution. During a speech at the Kennedy School of Harvard in December of the same year, I stated that Chinese people will remember Deng Xiaoping because he is the symbol of the CPC's initial focus on modernization and the beginning of a never-before-seen phase of development, both of which occurred during the reform and opening up as China became linked to economic globalization instead of economic separatism.

When the Asian financial crisis erupted in 1998, I gained a clearer understanding of the duality of economic globalization and the path China was on. At that time, I wrote, "We have already been on a bright path of independently developing socialism with Chinese characteristics while actively participating in economic globalization."[6] While leading instruction reform at the Central Party School and writing teaching mate-

[6] Zheng Bijian: "On grasping the big picture and China's theoretical program, and a great revelation regarding the Asian financial crisis," *Essays by Zheng Bijian*, Vol. 2, Shanghai People's Publishing House, 2005, Chinese edition, p. 621.

rial oriented toward the 21st century, I stated, "The world is undergoing a great transition, of which the major source is the economy. … The current, worldwide transition includes a transition in the theme of the times, the rise of a revolution in new technology and industry, rapid development in the world market and a huge transformation in the structure of the world economy. It also includes a consistent trend of multipolarity for the world and a new wave of economic globalization." I was able to say this as a result of what we had learned from the Asian financial crisis, this being the first time I spoke on the outlook for the new wave of economic globalization.[7]

As for how China developed itself during such global transition, I further affirmed, "Over the past 20 years since the Third Plenary Session of the 11th Central Committee, China has seized all available opportunities, proceeding along a new path linked to economic globalization instead of economic separatism while independently developing socialism with Chinese characteristics," and I consistently used this wording all along.

2. My proposal after Party congress: unprecedented path of peaceful rise for China

During the first CPC national congress of the 21st century (the 16th CPC National Congress, held in November of 2002), a major decision was made: to seize the opportunity of the first 20 years of the new century to create a "moderately prosperous society" (a term coined by Deng Xiaoping) for the whole of China. I was involved in drafting documents

[7] Zheng Bijian: "Conceived framework in *The Contemporary World Economy*," *Essays by Zheng Bijian*, Vol. 2, Shanghai People's Publishing House, 2005, Chinese edition, pp. 685-686.

for the congress and realized this was a huge part of Deng Xiaoping's Three-Step Strategy toward modernization. To practically implement this strategy, not only did the relationship between domestic reform, development, and stability need to be properly handled, but economic globalization and comprehensive national power-based competition (within the background of global multipolarity) had to be dealt with correctly so as to create a good international environment and open China up further to the world. It was precisely under such new conditions that research on the path of China's peaceful rise was made a priority for the daily agenda.

This is how it happened. In December of 2002 (after the 16th CPC National Congress), I left my post as executive vice president of the Central Party School and, as chairman of the China Reform Forum, went to the US to talk about the recently concluded congress. While there, I met people who held one of two views on China. The first was that, as a large country on the rise, China would inevitably challenge US strategic interests and thus be a threat to the US. The other view was that China would emulate the Soviet Union and eventually fall. With regards to these concepts held by much of the American government and public, while discussing the spirit of the 16th Congress and especially the path of development for the CPC during the 21st century, I stated, "China will proceed along a path that is completely different from the paths of development taken in recent history by other large nations: It will take a path of a peaceful rise." I stressed, "This path of ours is different from that taken by World War I Germany and World War II Japan and Germany, paths that called for invasion, war, and re-partitioning of the world; it's also different from the path taken by Brezhnev era Soviet Union that competes with the US for world power through military alliances and arms races."[8] In the several speeches I gave in the US, I clearly summed

[8] Zheng Bijian: "The 16th CPC National Congress and the new path for China's peaceful rise," *Essays by Zheng Bijian*, Vol. 3, Shanghai People's Publishing House, 2005, Chinese edition, p. 1122.

up the strategic path of China being linked to economic globalization instead of economic separatism while independently developing socialism with Chinese characteristics as a completely new path for China's peaceful rise.[9]

I, of course, felt the weight of this matter. When I returned to China (early January of 2013), I reported on my experience in the US to the the top leader and suggested that a research taskforce be organized as soon as possible. I thus initiated research that centered on this feature of China's peaceful rise. I further suggested that international forums on economic globalization and China's current path of a peaceful rise be held at an appropriate time. Leading departments regarded this suggestion as highly valuable, and on January 30, ordered research and, at appropriate time, exchanges with other countries on the issue to be carried out.

After that, I organized a number of meetings with personnel from the Central Party School and the China Reform Forum and visited related departments and officials at the Boao Forum for Asia. After diligent research, I submitted a report on the tasks at hand. In July and August of 2003, I formulated the outline for research, formed a core research team and subsidiary research teams, and organized experts (in and out of Beijing) in various fields to begin work.

Those in the subsidiary research teams worked tirelessly, and after four or five months of investigations, they wrote informative reports, such as "Comparisons of the Rises of Large Nations," "The Strategic Path of China's Peaceful Rise," "Concepts of an Era Based on Peace and Development," "International Strategies during China's Peaceful Rise," "The Rise of China in the Areas of Economic Power and Comprehensive National Power," "China's National Defense Development and Army Building since the reform and opening up," "The Youth of China

---

[9] Zheng Bijian: "New opportunities in the Sino-American relationship," *Essays by Zheng Bijian*, Vol. 3, Shanghai People's Publishing House, 2005, Chinese edition, pp. 1127-1128.

and the New Path for China's Peaceful Rise," "Strategies for Chinese Unity and Military Issues," "The Effects of China's Rise on Surrounding Countries and the World," "A Comprehensive Look at Sino-US Relations and Current Conflicts around the World," and "Well-reputed Overseas Experts and Political Leaders on the Rise of China." During this process, I hosted and attended a number of forums, such as project guidance meetings formed of senior members of the academic committee at the Central Party School. In addition, as suggested by leading figures, I initiated international exchanges on the subject of the path of China's peaceful rise at the Boao Forum for Asia.

The Boao Forum for Asia asked me to give a speech at its annual conference in 2003 to discuss this issue with political leaders and experts from other countries. In late October, I worked hard with those on my research team to draft the speech. In the speech, I stated that even though China had achieved a series of major advances, it was still an undeveloped country and still faced large-scale development difficulties. In talking about what "large-scale development difficulties" China faced, I used the metaphor of two simple math questions, one being multiplication and the other being division. The former was this: "No matter how small and thus negligible a difficulty for economic or social development seems to be, all you have to do is multiplying it by 1.3 billion to see how big it really is, and it may even be massive." The latter was this: "No matter how impressive the numbers seem for our financial and material resources, all you have to do is dividing them by 1.3 billion to see how low they are, and they may be depressingly low in per capita terms." The "1.3 billion" referred to the fact that the Chinese population was too large (and it still had not reached its peak, which is to be 1.5 billion around 2040 before beginning to decline). On the flip side, of course, this also implies increases in the areas of labor, innovation, and consumption, and the momentum of such is yet another order of magnitude! The development and rise of China include both difficulties and positive momentum, and in the end, both are inseparably related to the enormity of the Chinese population.[10]

After I gave this speech on November 3 at the Boao Forum for Asia Annual Conference, Secretary-General Long Yongtu of the Boao Forum for Asia said that the speech "possessed instructive significance for the whole conference." Ruan Cishan, the well-known commentator at Hong Kong's Phoenix TV, engaged me in a long, exclusive interview at the conference. In addition, Xinhua, *People's Daily*, China News Service, the *China Daily*, China Central Television, Hong Kong's Phoenix TV, and Hong Kong's ATV held a joint interview with me.

That Boao Forum for Asia Annual Conference was a success in many ways. First, the concept of the path of China's peaceful rise was

April 2005. Talking with former Singaporean Prime Minister Lee Kuan Yew during the Boao Forum for Asia

---

[10] Zheng Bijian: "The new path of China's peaceful rise and the future of Asia," *Essays by Zheng Bijian*, Vol. 3, Shanghai People's Publishing House, 2005, Chinese edition, p. 1175.

disseminated throughout China and the world, gaining attention from the international community and being seen as authoritative. Second was the systematic elaboration on the fact that China's rise is a peaceful one. That is, China has the complete capability to mobilize all proactive elements to resolve its large-scale development difficulties via support from domestic and foreign markets and resources while participating in economic globalization. Third was the elaboration on the relationship between China's peaceful rise and Asia, emphasizing that the peaceful rise of China is part of the peaceful rise of Asia, and that China will produce even more proactive and beneficial effects on the development, prosperity, and stability of its neighbors.

In January of 2004, we summarized the research and foreign exchange work we had done, and on this foundation, proposed the next phase of work.

Based on the project, in March of 2004, the core research team collected the reports from each of the subsidiary research teams and, by the following month, had put together the *Research Findings on the Path of China's Peaceful Rise.*

This 22,000-character report consisted of an introduction, a conclusion, and three chapters in the main section. The introduction explained the origins and development of the research. The first chapter of the main section summarized the path of China's peaceful rise over the previous 25 years, that is, the Chinese people standing up and beginning the march toward their national rejuvenation (which signified China's political rise) after the declaration of the establishment of the PRC. The path of China's peaceful rise that I speak of now, on the other hand, refers to the actualization of the national rejuvenation, which is a strategic path for a comprehensive rise during the period of time that began with the Third Plenary Session of the 11th Central Committee (in the late 1970s) and will continue until the middle of the 21st century with the modernization of China. The path of this peaceful rise is this: China is striving to attain a peaceful international environment for the sake of its own development, and it is making use of this development to maintain world peace. The essence of this is that during these times with peace and development as their theme, China is linked to economic globalization instead of economic separatism while independently developing socialism with Chinese characteristics, thus allowing China to be a stable force in maintaining world peace and achieving its rise.

The second chapter analyzed the opportunities and challenges China's rise would face during the first 20 years of the 21st century. Nineteen strategic issues regarding the dangers and challenges to China's rise were discussed. This chapter emphasized that it is wrong to think challenges will not be met with and to naively think that China's peaceful rise could happen smoothly overnight. Similarly, there would be no use if all seems lost and full of trouble and if opportunities are not seen, especially those masked by danger.

The third chapter elaborated on how the path of China's peaceful rise is a new strategy that has never been seen in Marxist history. The conclusion discussed China's peaceful rise and its relation to the CPC, stressing that the Party has confidence, competence, wisdom, and the means to lead China in this endeavor.

Leading departments attached great value to this report, and held a special meeting to discuss it. They thought that in the beginning, this research project was proposed because of the concepts overseas of the "China threat" and "the coming collapse of China." In essence, it was also to answer these questions: Can China achieve rejuvenation for its people as a developing country of 1.3 billion? How is this to be done? What will the effects be on the world? These are very important questions and needed to be seriously studied. They pointed to a specific sentence that they thought served as a perfect summary for the whole report: "China is striving to attain a peaceful international environment for the sake of its own development, and it is making use of this development to maintain world peace."

3. Nineteen strategic issues regarding dangers and challenges to China's rise

As stated earlier, the second part of the *Research Findings on the Path of China's Peaceful Rise* discussed 19 strategic issues. The main content of these issues is given below.

1. Whether China will always be able to maintain the impetus of reform to sustain strong development and ensure the national economy will continue to rapidly, harmoniously, and healthily expand.

Resolving all of China's problems relies on the crucial issue of development. We must rely on the impetus of reform to accelerate development, and we must be persistent with our scientific outlook on development to achieve faster, better development. Maintaining rapid growth for China's economy is inherently the greatest factor in economic security. The number of people added to China's employment population annually is no less than 14 million. If we do not have faster economic growth, we will be unable to solve the problem of employment. Furthermore, from the international angle, we must consider competition related to comprehensive national power: This competition is not only economic; it also implies competition among social systems and ideologies. If we do not gain the victory in growth and quality, it will be hard to convincingly prove to the world the supremacy of socialism with Chinese characteristics.

2. Whether China can ensure that the material and cultural needs associated with the continual population growth from 1.3 billion to 1.5 billion will be coordinated properly with resource, environmental, and productivity development.

An enormous problem for China's development is not only the formidable task of casting off poverty but also dealing with the arduous, limiting conditions of this task. China's large population with insufficient resources is a major factor that is holding back the nation's development. The amount of water possessed per capita in China is only one-quarter that of the global average; the amount of farmland per capita is only 40% of the global average; and the respective per capita reserves of oil, natural gas, copper, and aluminum are merely 8.3%, 4.1%, 25.5%, and 9.7% of the global averages.

Resource constraints are mainly in the areas of energy, food, raw materials, and water. This is especially true as China is currently in the middle phase of its industrialization, a time at which resources are depleted relatively quickly. Moreover, this is a time when the old and new forms of industrialization are overlapping, which makes resource constraints even more significant. Furthermore, China's production efficiency of resources is far lower than the global average. With the end of China's transition period of entering the WTO, ensuring long-term supply stability for strategic resources such as oil is going to be even more urgent. This is not merely an economic problem; it is a part of China's economic security and national security. We suggest the CPC Central Committee focus on China's resource constraints and energy constraints and put more into driving the revolutions in new technology, new industry, and production.

The Central Committee has already proposed measures to enhance energy production, lower energy consumption, and boost strategic oil reserves. Considering the importance and acuteness of the related current and predictable discrepancies, We suggest the Central Committee use a portion of foreign exchange reserves to comprehensively update old equipment that consumes large quantities of energy. We also suggest focusing on finding renewable energy resources by means of residential renovation projects in urban and rural areas, making improvements to people's living environments, and strongly promoting the use of solar energy among the general public while propelling the use of biogas in rural areas.

3. Whether we can guarantee the capital supply necessary to resolve China's large-scale development difficulties.

China is now either the world's largest or second-largest nation in terms of capital inflow, and it will remain so over the next few years. "Capital black holes" have become major concerns for the world, especially for developing countries, and capital flight is a lurking peril to China's development. After over 20 years of reform and opening-up, the people's savings have reached up to 11 trillion RMB, and if cash is also considered, the number is even more promising. How to adopt more effective measures so as to turn the people's money into capital (and thus reduce our reliance on foreign capital and lower our concerns about capital black holes) and curtail capital flight is a strategic issue related to whether China can peacefully rise.

We suggest related agencies carefully calculate their general and sub-accounts for capital supply, and on this foundation, accelerate financial reform. Moreover, on the foundation of boosting coordination between domestic and foreign capital, financial crisis early warning and management mechanisms should be established to ensure China's financial security.

4. Whether we can properly coordinate human resource development.

Accelerating China's modernization demands a "greater open

source," a focus on increasing the total number of workers and boosting their quality. By improving education and all other forms of training, we can turn the pressure of a huge population into the advantage of a large pool of competent human resources. The strength of China's comprehensive national power and capacity to sustain development is becoming more and more related to boosting the quality of the nation's workforce.

The dual mission of China's modernization demands that we continue to make use of our cheap labor to accelerate our new industrialization, all the while being very conscious and efficient in training up highly-skilled workers to drive informatization. The Central Committee has proposed a strategy of strengthening the nation through its workers, and on this foundation, we suggest we firmly grasp and establish the national program of "building a learning society." Moreover, it seems time we include the issues of population peaking, aging population, labor exports, and orderly immigration/emigration into our national development strategy so as to increase related research and find more solutions.

5. Whether we can accelerate development and maintain social stability while resolving the Three Rural Issues and propelling urbanization.

China has advanced from a per capita GDP of US$1,000 to US$3,000, this being a crucially important phase of development. There are two possible outcomes for the future: The first is that all is well and that the economy and society will continue to press ahead in development, allowing for a smooth path of industrialization and modernization. The second is that all does not go well: There could be a wide gap between the rich and poor, increased unemployment, greater urban-rural and inter-regional disparities, more social conflicts, and harm to the natural environment, all of which would bring about stagnant economic and social development and even social unrest and economic recession over the long term. We should seriously learn from the experiences of other countries that have gone through this phase. This is especially true because of China's current phase of development and its close relationship to the Three Rural Issues, the propulsion of regulated rural labor force flow into urban areas, and urbanization, all of which further complicate attaining stability for this phase of reformed development. In fact, social issues related to this phase of development are becoming more pronounced with each passing day, as can be seen by mass petitions, mass disturbances, and major incidents that have occurred in some places. We suggest the Central Committee organize resources to carry out research on problems associated with the early phase of socialism as was done in the past and, from the angles of theory and practicality, do in-depth studies on the problems of and strategies for the current phase of development. The findings may then be used to educate and train those in leadership.

6. Whether we can form a strong "cultural power" while participating in economic globalization.

The peaceful rise of China is comprehensive, and "cultural power" is an integral part. The cultivation of an ethnic spirit as proposed during the 16th CPC National Congress is very important to this. How to boldly borrow from the positive achievements of other civilizations (including those of Western capitalist nations) while efficiently curtailing "Westernization" and "disintegration" (including religious infiltration) via highly effective cultural innovation and while being involved in economic globalization, and how to strongly carry forward traditional Chinese culture while guarding against rigidity and outdated practices are a major test of the CPC's governing capacity. Our cultural innovation needs to aid in the formation of a rich spirit of the times while complying with Chinese tradition, thus propelling the strong cultural power of China's peaceful rise. We suggest that related agencies of the Central Committee firmly grasp and formulate a progressive program for a cultural buildup that embodies the characteristics of the times, is rich with the qualities of the Chinese ethnicity, and is tolerant. From this, first, we may continually drive the sinicization of Marxism through the development of a progressive, socialist culture and make use of this developing form of Marxism to guide its practical implementation. Second, it will allow for the practical implementation of boosting the general public's proper understanding of ideology, ethics, science, and culture as well as improving their health.

7. Whether we can continue to properly make use of the special advantages possessed by Chinese people around the world, forming a strong synergy to maintain world peace while driving development for all.

The tens of millions of people of Chinese ethnicity all around the world include those who have special advantages obtained by the massive introduction of foreign capital and technology into China during the early years of reform and opening up, as well as those who will ensure China's peaceful rise during the first 20 years of the 21st century. They are able to serve as messengers of peace in the political realm and are a link between China and the world to create an economic win-win for all involved.

8. Whether we can maintain China's sovereignty and security while participating in economic globalization.

Sovereignty is an irreplaceable foundation for the survival and development of a nation, and this will remain true for a long time to come. Economic globalization has made maintaining national sovereignty under new international conditions a more urgent and larger topic of study. Since the mutual interdependence between countries is continually increasing, many powers originally possessed by a single nation are gradually becoming shared by the international community, which has led to what is known as a "transfer of sovereignty." However, such transfer does not mean that one party may encroach upon the sovereignty of another country.

Within the process of economic globalization, a number of new situations and transformations have taken place in the realm of national security. Cooperative security has become an effective method in maintaining China's and the world's security. During China's peaceful rise, exploring new cooperative security modes based mainly on establishing measures of trust, especially in the aspect of establishing regional cooperative security mechanisms, has become a part of the daily agenda via international cooperation in maintaining national security. With continuing economic globalization, the scope of security is continually broadening to involve aspects that were not traditionally associated with security, such as the economy, society, the environment, and culture. Economic and cultural security are especially growing in prominence. We suggest that China take action as soon as possible to research and form a unified leadership organization for national security to formulate related strategies and establish early warning mechanisms and response systems for related economic, cultural, and societal security. This should be designed to ensure response measures may be carried out at any time against any threats to China's security and peaceful rise. The sooner this problem is resolved the better.

9. The peaceful rise of China and the question of Taiwan.

China's insistence on its peaceful rise is constructive to the question of Taiwan. The key to the solution for Taiwan will be decided by the speed and degree of China's rise.

Throughout China's peaceful rise, it is as the Central Government has emphasized: As long as there is a thread of hope, we must do all possible to unify the nation. Peacefully resolving the issue of Taiwan will be decided by: our persistence in the areas of economic and national defense development, for which we suggest a high degree of comprehensive national power; our conscious effort to win the hearts of the people of Hong Kong and Macao, maintaining prosperity and stability in Hong Kong within the "one country, two systems" framework; our effort regarding the people of Taiwan and boosting appeal for unity; our effort regarding the international community, especially in cooperation with East Asia (including with the people of Taiwan), so as to win the greatest breadth of understanding, sympathy, and support. Moreover, we must oppose and contain any claims or events that support independence for Taiwan, as there is no room for compromise here.

Giving the keynote speech at the 60-Year Cross-Straits Relations Seminar in Taiwan in 2009 as the head of the mainland delegation

10. The peaceful rise of China and building a strong national defense.

There is no question that China's peaceful rise requires a strong national defense to protect its strategic interests. Modernizing national defense is an important symbol of China's peaceful rise and ensures a strong backing for such pursuit.

Now that we have entered a new century and new stage of development, so as to guarantee China's peaceful rise, protect strategic corridors, safeguard overseas interests (which are escalating with each day), and participate in the international effort to maintain peace and combat terrorism, China must increase its investment into the military at the right time and to a proper degree, upgrading military equipment and promoting new military reforms so as to boost the power of our national defense. This is absolutely necessary and what is called for by the current conditions. As international competition is intensifying, it is especially necessary for China to study new strategies for national defense.

11. The peaceful rise of China and its relationships with large nations.

After the Cold War, and especially after the September 11 attacks in the US, a new wave in the relationships between the large nations of the world has emerged. The competition between unilateralism and multilateralism and the competition for international order has become a focus of conflict for large nations. However, in looking at the big picture, their cooperation generally outweighs their conflict as a new mechanism of coordination is forming. During the process of China's peaceful rise, the major direction being taken in relationships between the large countries is generally beneficial to China.

In handling relationships with other large countries, there is no doubt that China must guard against becoming encircled by the US and its allies while absolutely abstaining from joining or forming any sort of military bloc and refusing to become involved in spheres of influence of any kind. We must prepare a strategic and fully capable deterrent as a foundation for our will to persist with our peaceful rise but not look to become involved in an arms race. We must enhance the infrastructure of our "cultural power" but not become involved in forcing our ideology on others. We oppose hegemony but will by no means lead the fight against it. We have become clearly aware that China's rise will be up against hegemonism in politics, the military, economy, technology, and culture.

This is especially true of certain powers who oppose China and who will provoke and exert pressure on China with regards to such issues as human rights, Taiwan, Hong Kong, and trade. The differences and friction between China and major nations on a series of important international issues will continue to exist over the long term, and at times crises may even arise. We are also clearly aware that with regard to fighting international terrorism as well as maintaining world peace and Asia's stability and prosperity, there is a strong complementary relationship in terms of the numerous common interests and communities of shared interests (especially in the aspect of the economy) between China and the large, US-led Western nations. As long as we persist in focusing on our national interests and handle properly our relationships with other major nations by transcending above the differences in our social systems and ideologies, and as long as we seriously explore the creation of an early warning and crisis management mechanism, we will surely be able to build and expand common interests and communities of shared interests. This will drive development and ensure security for all involved while serving as a new concept for the peaceful rise of China and the handling of relations with large nations.

12. The peaceful rise of China and China's relationship with its neighbors.

China's relations with neighboring countries include two major aspects. The first is its relations with its large neighbors: Russia, Japan, and India. The second is its relations with ASEAN countries, neighboring Central Asian countries, Korea, and Mongolia. In recent years, we have experienced shifts in our relationships and promoted cooperation with large nations via developing relationships with small and medium-sized neighboring nations. We have also enhanced cooperation with small and medium-sized nations by balancing our relationships with large nations, and it has indeed worked well. On this foundation, pursuing neighborly policies to promote peace, wealth, security, and stability, we have further dispelled the worries small and medium-sized nations have had about China's rise. Thus, we have made use of the economy and culture to properly handle our relationships with our neighbors in the hope of creating a peaceful environment of reliable security, economic prosperity, mutual benefits, and long-term stability.

13. The peaceful rise of China and other developing nations.

Within the peaceful rise of China, advancing unity and cooperation with other developing nations is a basic foothold in China's foreign affairs. With regard to developing nations' misgivings about China's peaceful rise, China will by no means seek to dictate, and China always speaks up for them at large international events. Strongly driving economic and trade cooperation with developing nations that have resources and influence allows them to obtain benefits through China's rise and through cooperation and mutual support with China, thus allowing them to rise with China. Moreover, when conditions allow, China will increase aid to friendly African nations. In this way, China and other developing nations may make the best use of mutual support in handling major international issues.

14. The peaceful rise of China and international/regional communities of shared future.

The peaceful rise of China is certain to have an impact on the structure of power and interests in the international community. Furthermore, in terms of overall trends, economic globalization is linking nations to mutual interdependence. The related complexity demands that we actively promote international common interests, communities of interest, and communities of shared interests and challenges that benefit both China and other nations in various forms and on multiple levels during the process of China's peaceful rise. For example, the community of shared interests and challenges that responds to international crises and other global catastrophes and that holds economic interests as its core should make use of the existing "10 + 1" and "10 + 3" mechanisms (cooperatives between ASEAN, China, Japan, and Korea) while exploring free trade possibilities in Northeast Asia and between Japan and China. This would further enhance joint development, common interests, and communities of shared interests during China's peaceful rise.

15. The peaceful rise of China and a strategic resource passage network.

The development of economic globalization has led to a skyrocketing of imports of strategic resources into China, especially energy resources such as oil. For example, China is now the world's second-largest oil importer, and over 50% of that oil comes from the Middle East while about 80% comes through the Malacca Strait. Of the boats that pass through this strait, nearly 60% are either Chinese or en route to/from China. The fragility of such passage and China's nearly sole dependence on it implies the possibility of a serious economic and/or national security crisis. The US deployment of troops and related military behavior in the Malacca Strait area should seriously arouse our attention. As a result, China needs to think of a way to reduce its dependence on such strategic passages in the Western Pacific and accelerate the construction of multi-directional, multi-channeled land and sea oil pipelines. Oil pipelines are a core interest of China's economic and national security, partly deciding whether or not China will experience a smooth rise. As a result, we suggest related research begin as soon as possible so that China may plan from the big picture and manage the construction of a web of channels while working to ensure the free flow of traffic through strategic passages.

16. The peaceful rise of China and the issues of the South and East China seas.

A trend of "enclosure" is forming in the South and East China seas. This involves activity supported by the US and Japan that is disrupting China's strategic planning related to its peaceful rise, and it also involves the testing of China's bottom line with regard to its peaceful rise by neighboring countries thinking of their own economic and political interests.

The peaceful rise of China requires the establishment of a corresponding maritime strategy. China must maintain its rights over its territorial waters while holding to the overall concept of a peaceful rise, so such strategies must be particular. We must consider the fact that China's economy requires a large amount of ocean resources and consider the interests of related nations and joint development so as to work toward gradually developing common interests and communities of shared interests.

We suggest that the Central Committee continue in the existing direction that emphasizes respect of sovereignty, the laying aside of differences, and joint development in properly handling disputes. While maintaining basic stability in our territorial waters, we must adopt effective measures for the South and East China seas. I suggest considering the adoption of more favorable policies, such as discussing the possibility of jointly developing oil and gas fields in the South China Sea with large international companies so as to avoid being sidelined by the trend of "enclosure."

17. The peaceful rise of China and the issue of ethnicity and religion.

The issue of ethnicity and religion is an important part of building up a strong "cultural power" within the peaceful rise of China. It is an issue that must be properly responded to within the process of China's social transformation, and it is also an important aspect of rooting out the Three Evils (terrorism, separatism, and religious extremism).

The Chinese ethnicity has always maintained an attitude of harmony in diversity and has always looked upon everyone as being part of the same family while handling folk religion issues and while holding to developing and safeguarding the borders. The experiences of history must be learned from and made proper use of. A new feature has emerged with regard to the issue of ethnicity in socialism with Chinese characteristics: The diversity of benefits in ethnic minority regions, a boost in ethnic identity, strengthened religious orientation, and the imbalance in development between eastern and western China have over time brought relatively deep-seated conflicts and problems to the surface. These are obstacles to establishing an all-around moderately prosperous society.

We suggest that while maintaining the policies of regional autonomy for ethnic minority groups and religious freedom, the Central Committee continue to carry out in-depth research on the new features, trends, and functions of ethnicity and religion as related to the process of the peaceful rise of China. We should study the role of ethnicity and religion in China's push for strong "cultural power," correctly handle the social function of religion, support the proactive power of ethnicity and religion, strike down ethnic separatism and religious extremism, and eliminate the ethnic and religious foundation produced by terrorism. We must also place greater importance on implementing coordinated development measures in Xinjiang and Tibet as part of the international fight against terrorism.

18. The peaceful rise of China as it relates to the UN and other international organizations.

In this new century, we are faced with new challenges and opportunities. Ideas for large-scale reform are brewing at international organizations such as the UN. As the core of global order since the end of World War II, these international organizations are an active component of sustaining world peace, yet they are riddled with faults and deficiencies. The authority of these organizations must increase in terms of sustaining stability in the global order and the healthy operation of international mechanisms while preventing the strongest nations from carrying out hegemonistic strategies.

China's peaceful rise is linked to economic globalization instead of economic separatism and is part of equal cooperation and joint development with all nations. At this time of international competition between multilateralism and unilateralism, China upholds the former and works toward making full use of the UN and other China-friendly international organizations in the safeguarding of a stable and healthy international order. The peaceful rise of China, the joint rise of many other developing nations, and the appeal for equality and desire to develop of numerous developing countries are, together, a strong force in propelling gradual reform within international organizations.

We suggest we place importance on the core position in the current international order held by international organizations such as the UN, carry out in-depth studies on UN reforms, actively participate in UN affairs, and make full use of our permanent membership on the UN Security Council. We should actively participate in and support international missions, and when the time is right, promote and direct new, multilateral arrangements and the establishment of other international organizations as related to China's interests and territory.

19. The peaceful rise of China and international order.

Throughout history, the rise of large nations is always accompanied by the natural cycle related to maintaining or challenging the existing international order. The peaceful rise of China has transcended this long-standing rule, creatively progressing along a new path for a strong nation. Upon entering the 21st century, China must continue to progress along a peaceful route in its rise, handling the existing international order and international relationships by means of proper strategies and pertinent planning.

Currently, the international order is a prominent focus of international contention. The US method of seeking ubiquitous hegemony and pushing unilateralism is contrary to the trends of world peace and development of our time. China, on the other hand, works with other nations toward promoting the democratization of international relationships and making fuller use of the capacity of the UN in international affairs. In response to the disadvantaged position of developing countries in the current international order, China is actively promoting a new international political and economic order, advocating that regardless of a nation's size or strength, all nations should have legal rights and standing on the world stage. In brief, with regards to the current international order, China faces these questions: Should China adopt adversarial, non-cooperative methods, or should it make use of progressive, peaceful, democratic methods in participating in the reform of the unsound aspects of the existing international political and economic order? Should China, during its peaceful rise, choose to be the destroyer or insurgent of international order, or should it be a nation that works to improve and reform this order? We, of course, believe without a doubt that the latter is the correct answer.

These 19 strategic suggestions were put forward in 2004; reading them now, I still find them quite thought-provoking, especially certain domestic issues related to China's peaceful rise. Under the correct leadership of the Central Committee, effective measures have been adopted and have either led to issues being resolved or have initiated processes to resolve them. This proves that when the Party makes good use of opportunity in responding to challenges, it has the capacity to lead the Chinese people in achieving national rejuvenation and actualizing the modernization of socialism.

4. Expanding the influence of the path of China's peaceful rise

After that, we began to work in three areas: "in-depth research, regular exchanges, and an appropriate degree of publicity."

First, we continued to make use of the Boao Forum for Asia to expand the influence of the path of China's peaceful rise. At the opening of the forum's annual meeting on April 24, 2004, President Hu gave an important speech, stating, "China's development is inseparable from Asia, and the prosperity of Asia needs China. China insists on the path of a peaceful rise, holding high the banners of peace, development, and cooperation, working with the rest of Asia to bring revival to the continent and diligently making greater contributions for the sake of humanity, peace, and development."[11] After the opening, the China Reform Forum and the Boao Forum for Asia held a joint roundtable discussion to discuss the peaceful rise of China and economic globalization. In my address at the meeting, I talked about the path of China's peaceful rise and how it is a road that China indeed can progress along. I also spoke on what China's peaceful rise offers the Asia-Pacific region and the prospects for China and the Asia-Pacific region. A number of political leaders, experts, and entrepreneurs from the Asia-Pacific region and Europe attended the meeting, and they proposed numerous concepts of innovative value and asked many questions worthy of in-depth exploration. During the final meeting on April 25, I expressed deep gratitude for everyone's contributions and ideas. Noteworthy is that during the conference, I talked with former US President George Bush on the peaceful rise of China. Just after our conversation, he stated in his luncheon address, "The peaceful rise of China is a positive and important thing, and

---

[11] *People's Daily*, April 25, 2004.

all other Asian nations may rest assured."

In order to promote this new concept of the peaceful rise of China to the world, beginning in September, we put more effort into international exchanges. On September 3 that same year, I gave a speech entitled "Ten Points on the Path of China's Peaceful Rise" at the Global Summit in Europe. From September 28 to October 7, I led a delegation from the China Reform Forum and held 26 conferences and gave five keynote speeches in France, Italy, the Netherlands, and Belgium. During these exchanges, I candidly shared on three major challenges to the peaceful rise of China, namely, resources, the environment, and harmonious development between the economy and society. I also emphasized that China will transcend the old path of industrialization and the Cold War mentality.

Speaking at Stanford University during a visit to the US in 2011 (to his left: former US Secretary of Defense William Perry and China expert John Louis of Stanford)

We attended the Boao Forum for Asia for the third time in April of 2005. An international symposium was held by the China Reform Forum, Boao Forum for Asia, and the Asia Society on April 22. The vice chair of the NPC Standing Committee and president of the Chinese Academy of Sciences, Lu Yongxiang, and the deputy prime minister of Nepal's Council of Ministers, Bista, gave addresses at the opening. Singaporean senior statesman Lee Kuan Yew gave an address at the luncheon. A total of 150 people, including political leaders from various nations and experts from China and abroad, attended the event. I gave a keynote speech entitled "The Peaceful Rise of China and the New Role of Asia."

In an effort to better explain to the world the new path of development China has chosen, a white paper entitled *China's Peaceful Development Road* was drafted by related agencies of the Central Government and experts from the China Reform Forum in late August of 2005. I edited it at the request of agencies under the Central Committee.

While working on in-depth research from 2005 to 2006, we also carried out a large number of international exchanges. Of them, two important conferences must be mentioned.

One was The Path of China's Peaceful Rise and Sino-European Relations, held in Paris on December 6, 2005.

While in France, then Chinese Premier Wen Jiabao met with former Prime Minister Jean-Pierre Raffarin of France, former French Presidential Advisor Jérôme Monod, former Chairman of National Defense and Diplomacy Committee of French Senate Dominique de Villepin, and President Butler of the French nuclear power company AREVA. At the conference, Premier Wen gave a keynote speech. Since it was the Chinese Premier speaking on why China insists on a path of peaceful development, it was very effective at building trust and dispelling doubts. After the conference, I continued to lead my delegation in France, the Netherlands, Spain, and the UK.

By means of speeches, conferences, and conversation, we explained that "peaceful rise" and "peaceful development" are inherently the same, and that the peaceful rise embodies the characteristics of China's current phase of peaceful development. We explained that China's peaceful rise not only refers to rapid economic development but also advancing across-the-board the processes of coupling democracy with the market economy, coupling democracy with the rule of law; and coupling democracy with a boost in the character and thinking of our people and improvement for their lives. We further elaborated on the worries people have about the peaceful rise of China and the fact that the most essential aspect of this rise is the rejuvenation of Chinese culture.

The second conference I must mention was the China's Peaceful Development Road and the Future of US-China Relations roundtable discussion, which took place in Seattle on April 19, 2006.

This event was arranged to take place in coordination with President Hu's first visit to the US as the head of state from China. It was later apparent that this very strategic act had a strong effect on enhancing mutual trust and cooperation between the two nations, and numerous US think tanks placed great importance on this event. Strategy experts Henry Kissinger, Brent Scowcroft, William Perry, and John Hamre attended the event. President Hu met with them and all the other experts there, giving an important speech that aroused a significant response from those involved in US strategy making and US society at large. Kissinger, Scowcroft, Yang Wenchang (head of the Chinese People's Institute of Foreign Affairs), and I gave keynote speeches, and Perry gave the luncheon speech. Afterwards, I led my delegation to Los Angeles, Washington D.C., and New York, where I met with the Deputy Secretary of State Robert Zoellick, Senator Lindsey Graham, Justice Anthony Kennedy of the Supreme Court, President Jimmy Carter's national security advisor, Zbigniew Brzezinski, the former US ambassador to China Stapleton Roy, China expert David Lampton, and others. I also visited RAND Corporation and the Carnegie Endowment for International Peace. Furthermore, Li Junru of the China Reform Forum took some members of our delegation to San Francisco and Boston, where they met with former Under-Secretary of State Richard Cooper, John Louis who had taught former Secretary of State Condoleezza Rice, and China experts Ezra Vogel, Roderick MacFarquhar, Ramon Myers, and Tu Weiming. They also visited the Hoover Institution and Center for East Asian Studies at Stanford and the Fairbank Center for Chinese Studies at Harvard.

This event was very fruitful. In an address, I elaborated on three concepts: China's development is one of peace, the most essential aspect of this rise is the rejuvenation of Chinese culture during the first half of the 21st century, and the future of Sino-US relations is inseparable from exchanges and communication between these two great nations. In Kissinger's speech, he emphasized that we must understand the challenges faced by both nations and the fact that both nations are undergoing massive transitions. He further stated that the Sino-US relationship has

With former US President George H. W. Bush and his wife during the China Science and Humanities Forum in December 2006. Mr. Bush was invited by the author to speak at the forum, and presented the author with a copy of his book.

for a long time been quite extraordinary, and we should not simply focus on the present but also on the wonderful visions for the mid- and long term. Lampton stated that the biggest issue between China and the US is the mutual distrust with regard to strategy, and thus, we must seize the opportunity of constructive cooperation between the two nations to actively promote mutual trust. Perry suggested that the two nations establish a closer military relationship, for example, by beginning a collaborative effort in rescue and peacekeeping missions and engaging in military training exchanges. This would greatly enhance transparency for mutual trust.

These two conferences between the CPC and leaders from overseas and the resulting exchanges on a broad range of topics significantly increased the influence of the path of China's peaceful development and the path of China's peaceful rise on the international community.

Moreover, this series of events allowed me to become deeply aware that communication between cultures is an aid in the boosting of mutual trust. Thus, in my report on these two events, I suggested that the next phase is to intensify research on the path of China's peaceful development, expanding from the topic of our peaceful rise to the revival of our culture, and from a peaceful China to a China of culture.

5. The inclusion of the path of China's peaceful development in the Report to the 17th CPC National Congress and China's Constitution

It has been 15 years since the beginning of research on the path of China's peaceful rise began in 2002, and in looking back at this period of time in which those on my team worked overtime nearly every day, it is quite unforgettable.

What makes me especially happy is that our research and exchange events were not only strongly guided and supported by the CPC Central Committee, but all of the achievements we made were written into the 17th CPC National Congress Report in 2007.[12]

Section 11 of the 17th CPC National Congress Report discussed China's policies on foreign affairs. The title of this section was "Unswervingly Following the Path of Peaceful Development." The report stated that the world was in a state of major reform. While stressing the theme of the times was peace and development, he pointed out that global multipolarity is irreversible, economic globalization was developing in full gear, and momentum was accelerating for technological development. He also pointed out that China's relationship to the world was undergoing a historic transformation, and that China's future was day by day becoming tied closer to that of the world. In light of this, the report mentioned "two unswerving policies": The first was that China would continue to progress along its path of peaceful development, and the second was that China would continue with its strategy of opening up, forming a win-win situation for all involved. It emphasized that China would persist in developing friendships and collaboration with all countries on the foundation of Five Principles of Peaceful Coexistence, and stressed that China would continue to promote regional and global development by means of its own development, expanding converging interests in various aspects.

The strategic concepts and essential policies discussed in the 17th CPC National Congress Report gave us the direction in which to continue in our research on the path of China's peaceful rise and its implications for China's international relations.

"Following a path of peaceful development" was incorporated into

[12] The 18th and 19th CPC National Congress reports included "The Path of Peaceful Development" in the title for sections relating to the policies of the CPC on international issues.

China's Constitution as approved by the First Plenary Session of the 13th National People's Congress on March 11, 2018.

I would also like to add this: While being a part of all of the work mentioned above, my thoughts and study on the peaceful rise of China have continually intensified. An important aspect of this is that under the guidance of Deng Xiaoping's assessment of the theme of the times being peace and development, while researching the new strategic path of China's peaceful rise (or "development") within the overall topic of economic globalization, the strategic concepts of common interests and communities of shared interests formed. This point was already mentioned in this chapter, and will be further expounded upon in chapters four and five.

Chapter 2

Four Hundred Years of Economic Globalization and the Fate of China

We are concerned about economic globalization because it deeply influences the course of Chinese history while radically changing the world history. Today, a major task for us is to closely study the historical development and prospects of China's modernization and socialism with Chinese characteristics against the tide of economic globalization.

1. The first round of economic globalization and China's "Sunset Glory"

In modern times, China's tortuous journey with profound historical lessons has been inextricably linked to economic globalization.

Economic globalization does not appear all of a sudden but is the result of a fairly long process of development. Looking back at world history, the first industrial revolution, starting in Holland and Spain in the 16th century and ending in Britain between the mid-18th century and 19th century, can be regarded as the beginning of economic globalization, or, the first round of economic globalization. Marx and Engels's *Communist Manifesto* and other works contain the earliest descriptions of the appearance and characteristics of economic globalization.

The *Communist Manifesto* states: "Modern industry has established the world market, for which the discovery of America paved the way. This market has given an immense development to commerce, to navigation, to communication by land. This development has, in its turn, reacted on the extension of industry; and in proportion as industry, commerce, navigation, railways extended, in the same proportion the bourgeoisie developed, increased its capital, and pushed into the background every class handed down from the Middle Ages." "The bourgeoisie has through its exploitation of the world market given a cosmopolitan character to production and consumption in every country." ".... New industries no longer work up indigenous raw material, but raw material drawn from the remotest zones; industries whose products are consumed, not only at home, but in every quarter of the globe. In place of the old wants, satisfied by the production of the country, we find new wants, requiring for their satisfaction the products of distant lands and climes. In place of the old local and national seclusion and self-sufficiency, we have intercourse in every direction, universal interdependence of nations."[1] Based on the brilliant exposition of Marx and Engels, President Xi Jinping remarks: "Economic globalization is the tide of time that we must face in our strategic planning and development. Although the concept of 'economic globalization' became popular only after the end of the Cold War, such trend of thoughts appeared as early as the 19th century in the works of Marx and Engels, such as *German Ideology*, *Communist Manifesto*, *Economic Works 1857-1885*, and *Capital*, with detailed discussions on the issues of world trade, the world market and the history of the world." "These insights and expositions by Marx and Engels profoundly reveal the essence, logic and process of economic globalization and lay the foundation for our understanding of economic globalization today." [2]

However, the history of this large-scale economic globalization brought the Chinese people grave suffering and profound lessons. While chairing the work of the Central Party School, I organized the publication of a very influential article written by Professor Xu Weixin at *Study Times*[3]: "Sunset Glory." "Sunset" is the time when the sun is about to go down and the sky becomes spectacular and brilliant, comparable to sunrise. However, the sunrise ushers in a bright day, while the sunset leads to a dark night. The article talks about the fact that when the industrial revolution started from the United Kingdom and the booming economic

[1] Marx and Engels: *Communist Manifesto.*

[2] Xi Jinping: "Speech at the Seminar on the Guiding Principles of the Fifth Plenary Session of the 18th CPC Central Committee for Officials at the Provincial and Ministerial Levels," and *Selected Important Speeches of General Secretary Xi Jinping,* Party Building Books Publishing House and Central Party Literature Press, 2016, Chinese edition, p. 398.

[3] Run by the Central Party School, *Study Times* was first launched in 1999. Targeting leading officials at various levels and intellectuals, it is a newspaper especially on studying. Holding the theme of "Reading for Solving Problems," it is the CPC's only newspaper of its kind.

globalization brought mankind into a whole new era, the ancient China was at the Kangxi-Qianlong Heyday, a magnificent sunset forecasting a long night. In about 40 years after the "Heyday," Britain defeated the Qing Dynasty in the Opium War of 1840, a turning point when China was reduced to a semi-colonial and semi-feudal society. It is well understood that the defeat of the Qing Dynasty in 1840 was not accidental. The root of the decline had been planted during the Kangxi-Qianlong Heyday, a period of time governed by three great emperors of the Qing Dynasty: Emperor Kangxi (1662-1722), Emperor Yongzheng (1723-1735) and Emperor Qianlong (1736-1795). Under their more than 130 years of governance, the economy, culture, and all aspects of Chinese society had been optimized within the framework of the original system. By the end of the Qianlong reign, China had the largest economic output in the world, one third of the world population, long-term favorable balance of trade, and six out of the 10 world cities that had over 500,000 inhabitants. French enlightenment scholar Voltaire praised China as "the oldest, largest and the most beautiful and populous country under the best governance in the world." Another French enlightenment scholar, Diderot, in the entry of "China" of his supervised publication *Encyclopedia*, held high regards to the Chinese nation and viewed its history, culture, arts, wisdom, political and philosophical thoughts above all ethnic groups. "However, just under the glory of its primetime, the Qing Dynasty saw itself as "the great power of the heavenly kingdom," disparaged the science, technology, and inventions of the West as "sensational tricks and crafts," viewed market-oriented commerce and industry as "the endmost occupation," rejected free trade and commerce, and failed to promote the industrial revolution in China. As a result, China missed a major development opportunity – the worldwide industrial revolution and the first round of economic globalization. At a time when the tremendous productive forces brought by the industrial revolution and economic globalization transcended Western society, China remained stagnant with the late feudalism. Although the setting sun is glorious, only a quiet night follows.

This period of history gives us multifaceted warnings. Of the most importance was the decay and decline of the ruling class. In the face of such a huge and grave historical challenge, the rulers were first ignorant, and then fell from blind arrogance (one extreme) to knee-jerk surrender (the other extreme). As a result, China became a semi-colonial society under the gunboat diplomacy of the West and underwent over 100 years of suffering.

2. Two historical pursuits and three turning points of modern China

The Opium War of 1840 marked the beginning of the modern history of China. Since then, the history of the Chinese nation has been filled with incessant turmoil. China entered the 20th century with tremendous humiliation as capital Beijing was occupied by eight foreign coalitions in 1900. The national disgrace was shared and engraved in the hearts of the Chinese people.

When summing up the historical experience of China in modern times, the 15th CPC National Congress pointed out that after the Opium War, China gradually became a semi-colonial and semi-feudal country. Since then, the Chinese nation has faced two major historical missions: One is to seek national independence and liberation of the people; the other is to realize the prosperity of the country and the happiness of the people. To put it simply, the goals are "to save the nation" and "to rejuvenate and develop." And these two historic pursuits have become the greatest challenge for the entire Chinese nation, including all classes, political parties and their leaders in China, and the most profound impetus for many generations of unremitting efforts, from 1840 to 2050.

What needs to be pointed out is that the two major missions concerning the nation's future and rejuvenation originate from the major changes within China and around the world, and from the dynamic changes between China and economic globalization. History shows that major changes in China's society and the three major turning points in Chinese history are inextricably related to the significant changes in the world, especially the tortuous development of the three rounds of economic globalization. This is an important perspective in examining the China issues.

The first round of economic globalization and the first turning point in Chinese history. Strictly speaking, the first round of economic globalization began in the 16th century and flourished in the mid-18th century when China was in the "Sunset glory" of the "Kangxi-Qianlong Heyday," while the British industrial revolution was under way. The 1840 Opium War was precisely the year when the British domestic railway network was established. It is not coincidental that these two events occurred in the same year but evident that the completion of the industrial revolution in Britain marked the time when China was slammed into a semi-colonial society. Overall, for more than 100 years, from the mid-18th century to the end of the 19th century, due to missing the historical opportunities of the industrial revolution and economic globalization, China was outpaced by the times and gradually left behind, becoming the greatest victim of capitalism and colonialism. This is the first round of economic globalization and China's plight.

At the same time, in order to "save the nation" and "rejuvenate and develop," we had several visionary figures, such as Lin Zexu[4], who was extolled as "the first Chinese who opens his eyes to the world in modern times," and Sun Yat-sen, the forerunner who led the Revolution of 1911; they advocated rejuvenating the nation with unremitting battles. The Revolution of 1911 overthrew the monarchy that ruled China for thousands of years and ushered in the modern national democratic revolution. China experienced its first historic turning point. Although the Revolution of 1911 failed to change the societal nature of the old China and the people's miserable conditions, and failed to reverse the decline of the nation, it opened the door to progress and prevented the reactionary rule from ever stabilizing again.

The second round of economic globalization and the second turning point in Chinese history. This round of economic globalization began in the late 19th and early 20th century when capitalist countries entered the age of imperialism, a time when financial capital ruled.

However, the two world wars that lasted more than 30 years in the first half of the 20th century disrupted the progress of the second round of economic globalization and triggered successively Russia's October Revolution in 1917 and China's 28-year long New Democratic Revolution that began in the 1920s. Under the leadership of the Chinese Communist Party, the Chinese revolution took the opportunity during the halt of the second round of economic globalization. Led by the first generation of the collective leadership with Mao Zedong at its core, the Northern Expedition, the Agrarian Revolution, the War of Resistance Against Japanese Aggression and the War of Liberation, brought down imperialism, feudalism and bureaucratic capitalism. With the founding of

---

[4] Lin Zexu (1785-1850), born in Fujian Province, was a politician and thinker of late Qing Dynasty. As the imperial commissioner to Guangzhou, Lin suppressed opium trade by merchants from Britain and other countries, and destroyed illegal opium at Humen. Taking this as an excuse, Britain waged the Opium War against China. Lin Zexu is considered as a national hero due to his loyalty to the people.

the People's Republic of China, China won independence and the people were liberated, embarking the journey of socialism from the New Democratic Movement and obtaining tremendous achievements in socialist construction. This second historic turning point experienced by the Chinese people has opened the door to the two great historical pursuits in modern China. This is the second round of economic globalization and the chance for China.

The third round of economic globalization and the third turning point in Chinese history. This round of economic globalization began in the late 1970s and early 1980s when the United States failed in the Vietnam War and the former Soviet Union also suffered a setback in the war in Afghanistan. The global strategies of the two superpowers that could dominate a world war suffered major setbacks one after another; the world gradually entered a new period of time marked by peace and development. In particular, with the ever-changing science and technologies, the flows of information, capital and goods around the world have accelerated. Multinational corporations surge and the third wave of economic globalization has risen.

It was exactly this year, in 1978, the Third Plenary Session of the 11th Central Committee of the Communist Party of China decided to implement the policy of reform and opening up so as to foster China's socialist modernization. This was a new major revolution under the second-generation of collective leadership with Deng Xiaoping at its core. After 30 years of hard work and based on the historical experience, the Chinese people have successfully and independently blazed a trail to construct a socialist society with Chinese characteristics by catching up with, instead of separating from, the process of economic globalization. The path is the peaceful rise and development of China. The thriving vitality shown by socialist China during its reform and opening up has drawn the world's attention. This is the third round of economic globalization and the chance for China.

During these three rounds of economic globalization and the three turning points in Chinese history, the Chinese people have awakened to the decline of the "great power of heavenly kingdom," and realized they must overthrow the monarchy and establish a republic for a stronger nation. They realized that copying the Western path would lead them nowhere; only by carrying out new democratic revolution and catching up in arms could build a stronger nation. They also realized the Soviet Union's rigid model promised a dead end; they must take the road of socialism with Chinese characteristics, and implement reform and opening up. These are the three great awakenings of the Chinese in the past 170 years.

The combination of the external environment – an international situation full of ups and downs, and the internal force – an aspiration to save and rejuvenate the nation, has renewed the Chinese people's perception of the nation and the global trend through various major struggles as well as China's image and position in the world stage. In the face of economic globalization, we have the following options: One is to stay arrogant and separate from economic globalization and to pursue modernization behind closed doors. This has proven a mistake. Another is self-deprecating, willing to be vassals, and completely dependent on foreign countries. History has proved that this was tried and then failed. Only the third alternative, that is, by building socialism with Chinese characteristics independently through the process of reform and opening up, and staying connected to rather than separated from economic globalization, can we pave a unique path to success.

Chapter 3

A Whole New Strategic Path of Peaceful Rise in China's Reform and Opening Up

When China implemented economic reform and opening up policy, it was exactly when the third round of economic globalization emerged. Under the remarkable leadership of Deng Xiaoping, the Chinese Communist leaders seized this historic opportunity. First, they made a strategic assessment that peace and development have become the thrust of the times. Second, they formulated the fundamental guidelines: "One central task (economic construction) and two basic points (adhering to the four cardinal principles and the policies of reform, opening to the outside world and invigorating the domestic economy)." Thus they opened a completely new strategic path for peaceful development.

1. The rise and the historical features of the third round of economic globalization

Economic globalization has today become a controversial hot topic around the world. Different countries, different social classes, groups and various political parties, as well as politicians, economists, militarists and thinkers in various fields have participated in the discussion. Different schools of thought present widely diversified arguments. The direction of economic globalization in the early 21st century will have a strong impact on the overall international situation and even more so on China's domestic situation. Therefore, we will face major opportunities and challenges in the new century.

Generally speaking, economic globalization refers to the increasing interdependence of national, regional, and local economies across the world as a result of the growing scale of cross-border trade and market. As mentioned before, since the first industrial revolution, the world has already had three rounds of economic globalization. The following discussion will focus on the "third round" of economic globalization that extended from the late 1970s and early 1980s up to today.

So, how do we view this round of economic globalization?

First of all, just like the two previous rounds of economic globalization, this round of economic globalization is still the objective demand and ultimate result of the development of social productivity and is still dominated by the developed Western countries. The concept of "an era of economic globalization" was derived from America's "globalization era," which was used to supersede the "Cold War era" so as to represent the time during the Clinton administration. At the turn of the century, several "National Security Strategy Reports" issued by the United States use the term as the key word; or, as their guiding theory on national security at that time, the core idea is to allow investment and trade liberalization in the light of neoliberal diplomatic ideology in the context of the Soviet Union's collapse and the United States "superpower domination." It is also in the interest of the United States to maximize its unique position in the world as "a super-dominate" power. Its political orientation, in contrast to that of the Cold War era, is more toward the engagement of major powers rather than deterrence, more inclined toward international organizations and multilateralism than isolationism, and toward investment and trade liberalization rather than protectionism. Its policy is materialized through the global governance platform composed of the seven developed countries, namely G7[1] (and later for a while joined by Russia to become G8).

Therefore, this round of economic globalization is a "double-edged sword" for developing countries like China. We must guard against all kinds of risks that undermine national sovereignty and economic security; we may as well take advantage of the markets and investment facilities provided by free trade in the process of economic globalization. In general, this round of economic globalization is dominated by US design and conducive to US hegemony. Only after the 2008 global financial meltdown triggered by the subprime mortgage crisis in the United States did the internal structural contradictions and shortcomings of this round of economic globalization begin to show and the American "superpower

---

[1] G7 is the summit of the countries – United States, Britain, France, Germany, Japan, Italy, Canada – to study the economic situation and coordinate governance policies. Inaugurated in 1975, G7 has become a summit of the leading industrialized Western countries. A number of international action plans are reached in this framework. For example, in the political field, G7 reached agreement on the Kosovo war and the apportionment of related war costs at the end of the last century; in the economic field, the well-known Plaza Accord and the aid to the Southeast Asian financial crisis are also the fruits of G7 operation.

dominance" began to waver. And of course this was unexpected by the United States and the West.

Second, this round of economic globalization is characterized by the expansion of multinational corporations. The "multinational corporations" refer to those large-scale enterprises that have set up branches and subsidiaries overseas through direct investment and have formed industrial monopolies operating in the form of multinational organizations. Such companies emerged in the more economically developed US and European countries in the late 19th and early 20th centuries. However, by the late 1970s and early 1980s, multinational corporations had enjoyed rapid growth as the number increased to more than 10,000 with 100,000 foreign subsidiaries and branches under their control. By 1996, the number of multinational corporations had increased to 44,000 and the number of controlled subsidiaries reached 280,000. Their worldwide employees also grew to more than 70 million. By 2001, there were 65,000

April, 23, 2013. Meeting with former Australian Prime Minister Kevin Rudd at the CIIDS

multinational corporations with 850,000 subsidiaries and annual sales of US$19 trillion. In particular, multinational corporations control 40-50% of the world's industrial output, 50-60% of international trade, 90% of foreign direct investment and 90% of the world's technology transfer.

The emergence of multinational corporations means that the world market has gained unprecedented space for expansion. However, while transnational corporations are trying their best to gain maximum profit and vigorously develop the markets in developing countries, the economy in the developed countries is hollowed out and the unemployment rate in connection with it increases. As a result, social conflicts in the developed countries exacerbate. This is yet another thorny issue encountered by the Western developed countries in the domestic economic and social development during this round of economic globalization.

Third, this round of economic globalization was born in a historical context when peace and development became the main themes of the times in the late 1970s and early 1980s, a historical feature never seen before in the previous economic globalization. The first and second rounds of economic globalization finally led to various wars and eventually two world wars due to the colonial aggression of capitalists (first round) and the territorial division of the world by imperialists (second round). It was not until the Vietnam War and the Afghan war ended and when "peace" and "development" became the themes of the times that the third round of economic globalization began. This great historic shift in the world political landscape undoubtedly has created unprecedented favorable conditions for the liberalization of global economic and trade.

However, this round of economic globalization has not shaken off the Cold War mentality and retains the "dream of hegemony" under the dominance and design of the United States, especially after the drastic change in the Soviet Union and East Europe and the end of the Cold War. So here is an intriguing phenomenon. On the one hand, under the themes of peace and development, a multipolar world is emerging and expedites economic globalization. On the other hand, the developed Western countries headed by the United States have maintained their "supremacy" in system and mechanism, from economy to diplomacy. This is the most deep-rooted contradiction encountered during the third round of economic globalization.

Fourth, the rise and progress of this round of economic globalization is also closely related to the rapid development of science and technology, especially the revolutionary information technology. Information technology emerged during World War II. After the end of the war, industrialized countries such as the United States, Russia and Japan began to explore the application of information technology to the civilian sector. From the first appearance of electronic computers in 1946 to today's information superhighway based on computer networks and the advent of intelligent computers, human society is becoming an IT-based

November 5, 2011. Meeting with former German Chancellor Gerhard Schröder during his visit to Berlin

society. In particular, the Internet entering the people's life is not only a profound revolution in the field of science and technology, but also embodies another dawn of human civilization, marking a new era in human history. Internet is without doubt a tremendous driving force in accelerating economic globalization.

Of course, there is a flip side in this important area, that is, the developing countries are facing the technological blockade imposed by the developed countries, completely in contradiction with the trend of economic globalization and information society. At the same time, either the developing countries or the Western countries have enjoyed the benefits brought by the information technology; at the same time, they all have encountered the challenges on the issue of network governance. This is yet another special contradiction encountered in the development of this round of economic globalization.

2. China's strategic decision and great awakening

With regard to the third round of economic globalization, how can we Chinese Communists observe and seize the opportunities, meet the challenges and avoid complications so as to benefit the great cause of building socialism with Chinese characteristics? These have become the most fundamental issues that affect the outlook of our undertaking.

As mentioned earlier, China, which had missed the historical industrial revolution and the first round of economic globalization, started a revolution during the break of the second round of economic globalization and established the People's Republic of China. In the end of the 1970s and the early 1980s, China seized the strategic opportunity of participating in the third round of economic globalization and has advanced swiftly in the building of socialism with Chinese characteristics. And this is when China launched the reform and opening up under Deng Xiaoping's leadership.

Chinese Communists took a brand-new way of thinking of "[being] geared to the needs of modernization, of the world and of the future,"[2] by connecting China's development with the economic globalization of world economies, and thus opened up a completely new era in China. At the same time, the CPC has also taken note of the inherent contradictions of duality in this round of economic globalization and its challenges to such developing countries as China. On the basis of accumulated past experiences, the 12th CPC National Congress (1982) and the 13th CPC National Congress (1987) formulated the three-step development strategy to see that "the socialist modernization is basically realized." The 16th CPC National Congress (2002) also gave guidance to "grasp the important strategic opportunities in the first two decades of the 21st century" and formulated the strategic plans for building a moderately prosperous society in an all-around way by 2020. In this way, the first of the Two Centenary Goals would be fulfilled in time for the CPC centenary in 2021. After sustained and rapid development, China became the second largest economy in the world in 2010.

In review, such progress is not easy – as things are easier said than done. A critical issue here is to participate in and benefit from economic globalization while avoiding potential risks. The three essential guidelines to achieve this goal are as follows. First, the CPC soberly makes the scientific assessment that peace and development are the main themes of the times, grasps the historic opportunity of the shifting political landscape in the world, and draws the roadmap that is centered on economic construction and adheres to the socialist approaches and the leadership

[2] Deng Xiaoping: "Message Written for Jingshan School," *Selected Works of Deng Xiaoping*, Vol. III, Foreign Languages Press, 1995, p. 46.

of the Communist Party during reform, and formulates a foreign policy of peace and independence. Second, the CPC soberly makes a rational judgment that economic globalization is an objective requirement and an inevitable outcome of the development of social production. It seizes the historic opportunity of a new round of economic globalization by formulating a comprehensive opening up policy and participating in economic globalization while paying attention to major decisions to guard against risks. Third, the CPC soberly makes the rational assessment that the rapid development of science and technology is the trend of the times and seizes the historic opportunity with a strategic plan to promote a new industrialization that is led by IT-driven industrialization and industry-driven information technology and features high technologies, good economic returns, low resource consumption, less environmental pollution, and optimized human resources.

These three strategic decisions and guidelines boil down to this: China should follow the path of peaceful development, that is, China's peaceful rise. This path not only consolidates the fruits of long-term revolution, construction and reform but also realizes socialist modernization while taking a big step toward economic globalization. This is a great awakening demonstrated by the Chinese Communist Party and the Chinese people when facing the tide of economic globalization in today's new historical context.

This without question is a difficult yet imperative strategic decision. Under further examination, this strategic decision has the following attributes.

First, it is a challenge to independently build socialism with Chinese characteristics as well as to take the initiative in participating in the economic globalization led by the developed Western countries. An important step to participate in the economic globalization is to join the World Trade Organization (WTO), which necessitates arduous and even marathon-style negotiations with Western countries headed by the United States as well as the need to solve differences within the CPC in order to reach a consensus.

These two issues were jarringly placed before the Chinese Communist Party in the 1990s. Let's begin with the latter. At that time, there were two fundamentally conflicting thoughts in the domestic intellectual community. One argument said that China should pay attention to economic globalization and join the WTO. The other viewed that China must never participate in economic globalization or the WTO, because economic globalization was first promoted and dominated by the developed countries. In particular, the Asian financial crisis in 1997 proved that developing countries were unable to protect their economy under economic globalization.

The third generation of the central collective leadership with Jiang Zemin at the core fully listened to various views and carefully thought through the advantages and disadvantages of economic globalization in China's development. The leadership made the major decision on participating but seeking countermeasures. Jiang Zemin said: "Economic globalization is the objective trend of international economic development. This trend cannot be changed at one's will, and no country can avoid it. … At the same time, we must be clearly aware of the risks that economic globalization brings, maintain our independence and initiative, increase our level of vigilance, and become better able to fend off and defuse risks in order to effectively safeguard our country's economic security and better develop and strengthen ourselves."[3]

The challenges of that time are as follows: First, both inside and outside the CPC is under the influence of traditional thoughts; second, various departments and sectors have specific considerations, such as fear

[3] Jiang Zemin: "The Present International Situation and Our Diplomatic Work," *Selected Works of Jiang Zemin*, Vol. II, Foreign Languages Press, 2012, pp. 196-197.

of reduced tariffs on imported goods; third, relevant departments had no previous experience or enough competence to deal with international economic organizations such as the WTO; fourth, there were real risks, especially in our traditional agriculture and certain newly rising industries; fifth, some officials had not yet formed a visionary strategy, especially in terms of the correct grasp of the domestic and international situations; six, there were different views toward the understanding of international relations, especially the relations with the United States. And this was why the CPC Central Committee's decision to join the WTO and participate in economic globalization were met with different responses among scholars and officials. To solve this issue, the Central Committee also held seminars for major officials at provincial and ministerial level in the Central Party School to study the institution and related documents of the WTO so as to facilitate consensus-building.

The case also shows that China's development path of peaceful rise is by no means just a foreign policy but also a uniform guideline for internal and external affairs; it is by no means only about economic growth but also for a cohesive economic and social development; it is by no means applied only to science and technology innovation or economic reform but also to a unified reform of market economy, democratic politics, science and technology, and changes in the quality of the population. Or to put it more thoroughly, it is yet another great transformation of Chinese society in the first half of the 21st century.

Second, China's development path should surpass the old-style industrialization and constantly advance the development of a new type of industrialization, that is, IT-based industrialization.

After the start of modern industrial revolution, the entire world took 250 years to bring 1.5 billion people into the industrialized society. However, China has had to carry 1.5 billion people into the new industrialization, which drives as well as is driven by information technology, in the

100 years from the founding of the PRC to the mid-21th century.

Obviously, it is impossible to propel such a populous nation to develop without keeping pace with the progress of human civilization. If we again choose the old-style industrialization that requires high input, high consumption and high pollution, it is not going to work. In particular, China's modernization faces three major challenges: shortages of resources, environmental pollution and lagging social structure. China is determined to build a new type of IT-based industrialization featuring high technologies, good economic returns, low resource consumption, less environmental pollution and optimized human resources. China's strategy is to adhere to the development goal and build a moderately prosperous society in an all-around way. On this basis, first, we must further reform, promoting comprehensive restructuring in the economic, political and cultural fields; second, we must make overall plans for both urban and rural development, for regional development, for economic and social development, coordinate the harmonious development of man and nature, and make overall plans for domestic development and opening up to the outside world; third, we must maintain sustainable development.

Third, China's development path is different from the competitive approaches of the Western developed countries and the former Soviet Union.

The repeated history of hegemony of major powers in modern history has illustrated that the rise of a great power often leads to drastic changes in the international arena and the world order and even sparks a war. An important reason here is that they take a path that relies on waging a war of aggression to realize external expansion. Since such a path always ends in failure, it can never be the path of choice for China. China is a staunch force in safeguarding world peace and stability. China resolutely abandons the old approach of relying on wars to interrupt the world order or group's opposition to fight over hegemony but through the principle of democratization of international relations to establish a new international political and economic order, without seeking hegemony, taking the lead, holding dominance, nor acting as a vassal. In this way, we will be able to surpass both the fierce competition for resources resulting from the old industrialization and the Cold War mentality that rejects peace, development and cooperation because of ideological differences. Moreover, it is precisely during the process of economic globalization that various resources, including energy, can be brought in through the world market to fully mobilize the domestic and international markets and resources without having to resort to aggression and plundering abroad. In this sense, it can be said that economic globalization is conducive to China's peaceful rise.

Of course, as a developing country, China knows very well that the huge amount of capital, technology and resources needed for promoting modernization must be obtained from the world market through equal and mutually beneficial competition, yet without being overly dependent on world markets. Therefore, China has always paid attention to further opening up while relying on domestic-developed concept and system innovation, on its own industrial structure adjustment, on the development of an increasingly large domestic market, on turning huge household savings into investment, and on deepening the development of human resources, that is, raising the quality of the people and accelerating the progress of science and technology. These are the "five-dependence" solutions to the problems in the process of development. Therefore, we have every reason to say that China's peaceful rise is a unique path of modernization that is different from those adopted by Western developed countries and the former Soviet Union.

Fourth, in terms of the basic stance, viewpoint and approach of the CPC, the strategic planning of China's peaceful rise fully embodies the fundamental guideline on the basic issue of "what socialism means and how to build socialism."

As Deng Xiaoping clearly pointed out, the socialism we build is "socialism that develops productive forces and advocates peace." The Chinese people uphold this goal against a historical context that is marked by peace and development, which distinguishes China from the Soviet Union that supported hegemonism under the banner of "communism"; China thus establishes a new image of communists and socialism.

Fifth, the bottom line is that the peaceful rise is in itself a trend of the times. Over the course of the 40 years of the third round of economic globalization, there are three major changes that are beyond the strategic measure of the United States, leader of this round of economic globalization. These changes are as follows: First, with the collapse of the Soviet Union and the drastic changes in Eastern Europe, the world has not seen the "end of history" under the reign of capitalism; second, China's rise to participate in economic globalization does not mean China is "integrated into globalization," not to say completely westernized; third, as a result, the United States is in a state of decline and China is on the rise to become the world's second largest economy; fourth, in today's world, not only China but also a group of developing countries are on the peaceful rise. The fact is China's peaceful rise is only a part of the peaceful rise of Asia. The peaceful rise of Asia, especially the East Asia and South Asia, is already providing a powerful impetus to the world economy. Compared with the world's three major economic zones, the East Asia Economic Zone with the core of "10 + 3" has the most growth potential. At the same time, Asia has the largest population and the most dynamic emerging markets in the world. The total population of China, India, Southeast Asia and other South Asian countries, together amounts to about 3 billion, accounting for about 50% of the world's total population and about 65% of the population of developing countries. Asia not only provides the most important solution to the development problems but also possesses an emerging market with great potential for development. Accelerating the development of Asia and realizing the peaceful rise of China will provide the possible solutions to the most difficult problems of peace and development encountered in the contemporary world.

In addition, the peaceful rise of Asia, especially East Asia and South Asia, has provided new experiences and new models for the peaceful coexistence between countries and regions of different systems and cultures in the world. A series of non-traditional security crises that have taken place since 1979 show that the various objective forms of cooperation between our East Asian countries have been and will be surpassing the social systems and ideological differences in various East Asian countries. Of course, it is undeniable that there are still many hot issues and historical disputes in this region. However, we believe that politicians and people in East Asia are smart enough to find a solution by consensus instead of imposing on others, bridging disagreements rather than creating troubles, and building self-improvement instead of injustice. It should also be pointed out that such regional cooperation does not exclude the interests of the United States and the EU in Asia. On the contrary, under proper conditions, the United States and Europe will gain more from the rise of China and the cooperation in East Asia. The peaceful rise of China and Asia has provided an increasingly broader market for the international community, including the United States and other developed countries.

We are pleased to see that in the world in the first half of the 21st century, a large number of developing countries are moving toward peaceful rise through different paths, models and paces. At the same time, the developed countries are also seeking new major redevelopment in the new round of modernization. At both ends of the Eurasia, the rise of East Asia, South Asia and Europe is gaining momentum. This is a major new trend of peace and development in the contemporary world and should be greeted wholeheartedly.

The following few pages are a review of the history and tortuous journey of China's WTO accession with a focus on the marathon-like negotiations with the Western countries, especially the United State.

This work began in November 1995. Prior to this, the Chinese government had already proposed in January 1986 to restore China's position in the General Agreement on Tariffs and Trade (GATT), the predecessor of the World Trade Organization (WTO) and conducted numerous negotiations in the following nine years. To join the WTO, China's relevant departments first conducted 10 rounds of bilateral consultations with the United States and then went to Geneva in March 1996 to hold consultations with the WTO and its members. By October and November 1997, China had basically concluded bilateral market access negotiations with the vast majority of WTO members. However, the negotiations with the United States were the most intense. Following is the timetable of the negotiations with the US.

In October 1997, President Jiang Zemin, during his visit at the invitation of the United States, reiterated in his joint statement with President Clinton the acceleration of China's accession to the WTO.

On June 17, 1998, Jiang Zemin stated the three principles of China's accession to the WTO when interviewed by the US media: (1) WTO was incomplete without China's participation. (2) China undoubtedly wanted to join the WTO as a developing country. (3) China's accession to the WTO was based on the balance of rights and obligations.

On November 16, 1998, when Jiang Zemin and US Vice President Al Gore met at the APEC conference in Kuala Lumpur; both sides expressed the hope to conclude the bilateral talks early in 1999.

On March 3, 1999, a Sino-American high-level trade delegation stayed up late into the night negotiating tariffs reduction and further opening up in agriculture, telecommunication, finance and insurance sectors.

On March 15, Premier Zhu Rongji, at a press conference, noted that China had been engaged in WTO negotiation for over 13 years and that black hair had turned into grey hair. He expressed that it was about time to conclude the negotiation. He suggested that the current good opportunities should not be missed. First, WTO members acknowledged that without the participation of China, it meant that the WTO was not being fully representative and a potential largest market, China, was being neglected. Second, China's further reform and opening up and the accumulated experiences had given China the understanding of the likely regulatory capacity and affordability in the event of China's accession to WTO. Therefore, China would make the biggest concession necessary to join the WTO.

On April 13, 1999, US President Clinton and Primer Zhu Rongji agreed over the phone that two sides should conduct intensive negotiations to resolve the remaining issues concerning China's accession to the WTO.

On September 11, 1999, at a meeting with Clinton, Jiang Zemin remarked that China had always been positive about joining the WTO. China's accession to the WTO was not only necessary for domestic economic reform and development, but also for establishing a complete and open international trading system. China hoped negotiations could be conducted on the basis of equality and mutual benefit so as to reach an agreement as soon as possible. Clinton expressed his support of China's accession to the WTO and hoped to conclude the bilateral negotiations as soon as possible with further efforts from both sides. China and the United States reached an agreement on China's accession to the WTO on November 15, 1999. This signaled China and the United States officially concluded bilateral negotiations.

On June 14, 2001, after 66 months since the first negotiation in November 1995, China and the United States finally reached a comprehensive agreement on how to resolve the remaining issues related to China's accession to the World Trade Organization.

From 12 to 17 September, 2001, the 18th conference of the WTO China Working Group held in Geneva adopted multilateral documents on China's accession to the WTO, which had been submitted for consideration, and finally announced that the work of the Chinese Working Group came to an end.

On November 10, 2001, the WTO's fourth Ministerial Conference held in Doha reviewed and voted for China's accession to the WTO.

On November 11, 2001, in Doha, Chinese Minister of Foreign Economic Relations and Trade signed China's WTO Accession Protocol, which specified China's rights and obligations as a WTO member.

On November 20, 2001, exactly six years after the inaugural negotiation with the United States in November 1995, WTO Director-General Michael Moore sent letters to WTO members announcing that the Chinese government had accepted the "Protocol on China's Accession to the WTO" on November 11, 2001. When the protocol entered into force on December 11, China became the 143rd member of the WTO.

After nine years of negotiations to restore GATT and six years of negotiations to enter the WTO, it took China 15 years to participate in economic globalization.

This timetable paints a clear picture of the challenges China had experienced to take part in economic globalization. As a result of this effort, China has enjoyed 10 years of rapid development after accession to the WTO. Under the leadership of the Communist Party and with the hard work of all the people, socialism with Chinese characteristics has taken shape and China has quickly become the second largest economy in the world. In the meantime, we did not have the most taxing issues like economic security happen in the process of economic globalization, and we entered the Group of 20 and participated in global economic governance after the international financial crisis because of our mental preparedness to guard against risks and the countermeasure strategies.

Then, what is the significance of China's peaceful rise during the course of reform and opening up to the world?

First, China's stability is a contribution. Deng Xiaoping emphasized on many occasions that if China, a big country with a population of more than 1.3 billion, could not maintain stability and sent out refugees not by millions but tens or hundreds of millions, it would be a worldwide catastrophe! Any responsible politician should take this question seriously. Therefore, to maintain stability in time of major reform is a solemn attitude toward the world and a responsibility to mankind.

Second, China's reform and development are even more of a contribution. China's reform and development have enabled China to provide more products to the world and made China a greater market for the world. This is conducive to the prosperity of China and of all countries competing in the Chinese market.

Third, China's peaceful development contributes to world peace. China is a responsible major country and a devoted power in safeguarding world peace. China is also a major contributor to the world's peace and development. Against the historical context, China is never the initiator of the Cold War mentality but, on the contrary, the victim of such mentality. Therefore, China is even aspired to abandon ways of thinking and behavior that do not accord with contemporary thinking. After having suffered so much from the threats and humiliation of the big powers for generations, China has grown to oppose being threatened or threatening others.

On a side note, in modern times, China was once backward and exploited for not catching the "ride" of the industrial revolutions that transformed Europe and the United States. China's arrogant past that regarded foreigners as "barbarians" has been ridiculed and punished by history. So it is that today, some Westerners cannot accept China's rejuvenation because they have been accustomed to view China as a poor and weak country. When they regard a better off China as a "threat," isn't this some sort of outdated arrogance that needs to be examined?

Thus, it should be said that in the past, starting from the basic national conditions of China and leading the people in opening up a unique revolutionary path to encircle the cities with rural areas was a great awakening of sinicized Marxism. Today, starting from both the internal and international situations, confronting the tide of economic globalization and adhering to the goal of peaceful rise in reform and opening up is another great awakening of sinicized Marxism.

3. "Peaceful" – an answer to "the China threat," and "rise" – countering "the coming collapse of China"

At a time when the tide of economic globalization is rapidly pushing forward, China has always adhered to the strategic path of peaceful rise. The Chinese Communists have also demonstrated the wisdom at seizing opportunities and the courage to take on challenges.

What needs to be noted again is that the "new strategic development of China's peaceful rise" we are talking about is essentially the same thing as "China's peaceful development." In my writings and speeches, these two terms are often interchangeable. If there is any distinction, I have mentioned that "the development of peaceful rise" refers to China's peculiarities during the specific historical period from the initiation of reform and opening up to the realization of socialist modernization in the mid-21st century. "The path of peaceful development" refers broadly to the distinctive features of the entire history of socialism with Chinese characteristics, the promotion of development through peace, and the maintenance of peace through development.

Here, we should also clarify an issue – "China's peaceful rise" not only embodies the essence of "China's peaceful development," but also reveals its most distinctive characteristics of the times in addressing the cacophonies of "the China threat" theory and the theory of "the coming collapse of China."

Meeting with then US President George W. Bush at the White House in 2005

When American President J. W. Bush first took office, he regarded China as a strategic competitor. Especially before the "9.11" incident, there was a heated debate between the "red team" and "blue team" in the United States on how to face the rise of China. Most Americans recognized and worried about the rapid rise of China as a major emerging power. Against this background, such theories as "the China threat" and the "coming collapse of China" spark discussions in global community and invoke questions on China's peaceful rise in the course of reform and opening up. For example, American authors Bernstein and Munroe in their *The Coming Conflicts with China* promote the so-called "threat" based on the following reasoning: (1) China, the world's most populous nation, is a "potential superpower"; (2) China's economy will be the largest in the world in several years; (3) China is accelerating its military modernization; (4) Chinese nationalism is on the rise; (5) China is trying to dominate Asia; and in the next or two decades from now, China for sure will dominate the Pacific. These represent some Americans' view of China and their perception of its rise. What is the conclusion? "As a result, conflicts between China and the United States have even led to military confrontation between the two sides." This is the origin of the "the China threat" theory and its antithesis "the coming collapse of China."

The point is that China has pursued a path of peaceful rise, in which, "peaceful" is to counter the "China threat" theory, while "rise" is to counter the "collapsing of China" theory. This issue was specified as early as April 22, 2004 when the leading departments concerned discussed our study report.

Let's first talk about "the China threat" theory.

This argument has a long history. Ever since China carried out large-scale socialist construction, especially since its reform and opening up, whenever China attains new achievements, there is always someone voicing "the China threat." In the 21st century, the latest version for this theory is the "Thucydides Trap."

Thucydides (Greek Θουκυδίδης) was an ancient Greek historian. His masterpiece, *History of the Peloponnesian War*, consisting of several separate yet rigorously cohesive parts, gives a detailed account of the Peloponnesian War between Sparta and Athens, which were parts of the then powerful Greek Empire. The rapid rise of Athens in the 5th century BC shocked Sparta, the ruling power of the Peloponnese. The Spartans reacted strongly out of fear. The two sides moved from competition to confrontation, clashed, and waged a 30-year war that finally destroyed both of them. Thucydides concluded the book with the following statements: "At the time of the war, I began to write this historical book and believed this war would be a great war worth documenting more than any other war that had taken place in the past. And my faith is based on the fact that both sides had made every effort to prepare for it, and at the same time I saw the rest of the Greek world participate either on this side or on the other side; even those who at present haven't participated in the war are preparing for the war. This is the most serious turmoil in the history of the Greeks that also affects most non-Greeks. It can be said that almost all mankind will suffer from it." In short, what the "Thucydides Trap" emphasizes is that in the political reality, the fatal combination of strategic judgment and emotions between the two greatest powers would turn healthy competition into a rival of life and death over time, even leading to war.

People remember this and have found that since 1500, there have been 16 cases of a rising power challenging the existing ruling ones, of which 12 resulted in wars. Germany made a prominent case. In 1914 and 1939, the conflicts between Germany and Great Britain led to two world wars. In Asia, the rapid rise of Japan after the "Meiji Reform" challenged the order established or to be established by European countries in Asia; when intending to establish itself as the center of the Asian order, Japan started the Pacific war by invading other Asian countries in the name of resisting Western powers. Therefore, for many people, the "Thucydides Trap" is an inextricable spell. The newly rising power is destined to challenge the existing great powers, and the existing major powers must respond to such threats. The war is inevitable. The "Thucydides Trap" has become a catchword these days. Of course, their focus is not on history but on the China-US relationship such as "China and the United States heading toward a war."

In fact, when we proposed, "China should take a strategic development of peaceful rise," we emphasize that this is a completely new path of development that is different from that of the previous rising powers. We emphasize that China will break the myth that "a strong country must seek hegemony" and that a powerful China is not a threat but an opportunity to the world. On January 22, 2014, the inaugural issue of the American *The WorldPost* published Chinese President Xi Jinping's speech delivered on the occasion when met with foreign guests attending the "Read China" international conference. In addressing the current concern about China's rapid rise and its potential threat to the ruling powers, Xi said that all countries should strive to avoid the "Thucydides trap." The claim that the powerful country can only pursue hegemony does not

The First Understanding China Conference in Beijing in November 2013

apply to China, and China does not have the nature to carry out such an action. This is because the rise of China is a peaceful rise that will not start a war with the United States. The reason why China can achieve "peaceful rise" is that the Chinese people believe in "harmony is the essence to any relationship," and that "treat others as you want to be treated." In particular, China has formed a community of shared interests and future with all countries, including the United States, in economic globalization. Both China and the United States will benefit from a harmonious relationship. Therefore, upholding the principle of "peace," adhering to the belief in "peace," abiding the law of "peace" and insisting on the foreign policy of "Five Principles of Peaceful Co-existence," these are the best answer to "the China threat" theory.

December 20, 2017. Meeting with Graham Allison, founding dean of the Harvard Kennedy School, at the CIIDS

An additional note, on December 20, 2017, I had a frank conversation with Professor Allison of Kennedy School at Harvard University in Beijing. Professor Allison coined the phrase Thucydides Trap. He explained that this was not to advocate "war between China and United States," but to express his concern. I agreed and pointed out that since China and the United States fought against each other before – during the Korean War and the Vietnam War, both sides know the weight of war. And it was exactly after the Vietnam War ended and the United States withdrew from Vietnam, "peace" and "development" became the theme of the times. In my opinion, there are three options for Sino-US relations. First, "Eventually, it will get better," as Deng Xiaoping pointed out in his conversation with US General Scowcroft, a special envoy to China; second, "It cannot be very good while it will not get very bad either." This is a phrase commonly used in the diplomatic community; third, "there is bound to be a war," which is called the "Thucydides Trap." I also mentioned that the first option is the best and most attainable that both sides should strive for. The second option is nothing but procrastination, which is acceptable. The third option is something we must try our best to avoid. However, if the Americans want to fight, the Chinese will have no choice but to comply, as has been seen in history.

Next, let's talk about the theory of "the coming collapse of China."

This idea has been around even longer, probably since the founding of the PRC. It is always there and can be heard from time to time since the implementation of reform and opening up. In the past, the idea mainly criticized China's political system, human rights issues, stagnant economy, and the forecasted "collapse" of the communist regime. Now that it continues denigrating China politically, there are new versions and new bases such as: China's economy has now plunged into a "Latin American trap" or a "middle-income trap," so sooner or later the communist regime will collapse.

I think reality has already answered this argument. The so-called "Latin American Trap" refers to the rise of modernization after the independence of such nations as Brazil and other Latin American countries in the 1970s. In the process of modernization and urbanization in particular, they have seen more serious unemployment, wealth disparity, polarization, environmental degradation, insufficient public services and other social issues. What followed was increasing numbers of illegal activities, violence, and riots, and deteriorated public safety, thus affecting economic development. Now, decades have passed, but most of Latin America is still struggling, as if falling into a trap. Scholars name this phenomenon "Latin American Trap" or "Middle Income Trap." Almost all late-comers in modernization attach great importance to this phenomenon, which is regarded as a warning sign for the developing countries in pursuing modernization.

So, what has happened in China? The reality is that China's per capita GDP has exceeded US$8,000 and the nation has not fallen into the "middle income trap." Of course, at the same time, the Chinese Communist Party has realized that some imbalances indeed exist in the process of rapid modernization. These include imbalances in income between members of the society, imbalanced development between regions, and imbalances in economic and social development. These problems are related to the deep-rooted conflicts and problems in Chinese history as well as to the new developments that have taken place since reform and opening up. But in general, these "imbalances" and "widening gaps" are not "polarization" as some people name them. "Polarization" means that the rich get richer and the poor poorer. However, the "imbalances" and "widening gaps" that have emerged during reform and opening up refer to the fact that the overall incomes of all groups of people have increased but the increases are of different degrees. The key is that our Party and government have attached great importance to and have been dedicated to solving these problems. While some people are getting better off, the "minimum living standard policy" has been formulated in urban areas; and "poverty alleviation" and "poverty reduction" have been unswervingly implemented in rural areas. Especially after the 18th CPC National Congress, under the leadership of the CPC Central Committee with Xi Jinping at the core, the government has carried out poverty alleviation, trying to assist and reduce poverty with targeted measures. The Chinese government aims to "fight hard to win the war against poverty and help lift out of poverty all rural residents falling below the current poverty line, and achieve poverty alleviation in all poor counties and areas" by 2020 as well as to achieve reducing the poverty population by 10 million annually. In the meantime, a series of major policies such as coordinated development between regions, people-oriented new urbanization, and expanded public services to the whole society have been implemented. These are all efforts that have been made to avoid the "Latin American trap."

At the Central Conference on Economic Work, December 18, 2015, President Xi Jinping pointed out: "We must escape the Thucydides Trap and the middle-income trap. The former is related to political sphere – we should carefully tackle the relationships with other major countries such as the United States. The latter is about the economy – we must improve the quality and effectiveness of economic growth."[4]

Later, he also said, "The lesson of the international community, especially Latin American countries, shows that populism is the cause of the middle income trap. It has two prominent features: first, the blind pursuit of political democratization; with mixed views, and unable to

---

[4] Xi Jinping: "Improve Current Economic Work by Implementing the Guiding Principles of the Fifth Plenary Session of the 18th CPC Central Committee," *Selected Important Speeches of General Secretary Xi Jinping*, Party Building Books Publishing House and Central Party Literature Press, 2016, Chinese edition, p. 304.

concentrate on major issues; second, excessive welfare; with excessive commitment to please the public, resulting in inefficiency, growth stagnation, inflation, and increasing income disparity. We must start with the reality that income growth must be based on the improvement of labor productivity and that the raise of the welfare level must be based on the sustainable growth of economy and financial resources."[5] These statements made by President Xi Jinping provide the basic idea of avoiding the "two traps" in China and clarify fundamentally why China must adhere to the development path of peaceful rise.

4. "Duality" all the way – a tortuous journey

"Duality" is an important concept and should be an important study measure. For example, the economic globalization we are discussing now has "duality," and the economic globalization dominated by the developed countries such as the United States has even stronger "duality."

First of all, we must be fully prepared for the serious consequences that might be caused by out-of-control or badly out-of-control economic globalization; by the serious expansion of the North-South gap; by US hegemony and other serious local conflicts. The discussion here will focus on the economy only, without involving political or military considerations. In the 21st century, propelled by science and technology, economic globalization will certainly accelerate. However, US dominance will surely be further weakened. The international economic contradictions under the domination of the developed capitalist countries of the United States and Western countries will inevitably further deepen, intensify, and cause more turmoil and chaos as economic globalization

[5] *Ibid.*, p. 325.

progresses. The imminent problem is that the instability in international financial and economic development will increase. As the virtual economy is growing farther away from the real economy, it will inevitably lead to unpredictable risks. Since the early 1980s, when the US-led Western countries relaxed their control over the financial industry, a large amount of private capital flowed across borders and the exchange rate fluctuated. This in turn brought about various financial derivatives. Robert Mundell, winner of the Nobel Prize in economics, makes the following assessment: "The greatest danger to current world prosperity is the volatility in the exchange rates between the US dollar, euro and the yen." It is also estimated that the market cap of the United States, Europe and the Japan adds up to several trillions of dollars, while that of developing countries' totals less than US$2 trillion. This sharp contrast of 20-to-1 disparities is another important element in the possible systemic crisis. Only one percent of US assets reallocated will be enough to overthrow many emerging stock markets, resulting in asset bubbles and severe turmoil. Therefore, the World Bank also warned in its *Global Development Financial Outlook* that over the next decade, "capital that flows to emerging market countries may once see steep climbs, accompanied by the highly volatile and potential risks in the financial markets."

Given all of the above, we should have a better understanding of economic globalization in that risks do exist, so do benefits. Although not in a favorable position, China already has a solid foundation. Since economic globalization has become a reality, China will become even more backward if staying away from it. Therefore, taking the initiative to participate, seeking advantages and avoiding disadvantages, making the most out of the situation and riding on the momentum, is the right strategy.

Second, we must be fully prepared for the special complexities that our undertakings, including the great cause of building socialism with Chinese characteristics, are facing at the initial stage of socialism. The initial stage of socialism is actually an underdeveloped stage. It is precisely because of the underdevelopment that our mission at this stage is of special complex "duality."

For example, we need to free up the productive forces through economic restructuring that takes the socialist market economy as the orientation, promotes public ownership as the mainstay, and includes various forms of ownership economy; we also need to promote social justice to realize common prosperity.

Again, we need to promote urbanization as well as to give back to and revitalize the rural areas. We must support the continued development of the east as well as the development of old industrial bases in the central and western regions and northeast China. We must continue encouraging some people to become prosperous first while paying more attention to the low-income groups. We should not only continue emphasizing efficiency but also pay more attention to social equity. We must accelerate development while protecting the environment.

So the two sides of these issues are essentially unified but may contain contradictions in some specific areas. They might seem unified in long-term development, but contradictory in certain stages of that development. In other words, we cannot just focus on the one and ignore the other. That is why it is called a "dilemma," which can only be gradually resolved in a longer process. This requires a clear understanding of the duality and continuation of the issues as well as a grasp of the "measures" in handling the issue.

In other words, we must not divide the "dual missions" but strive to make overall plans for both. We must also not attempt to handle everything at one stroke. Instead, we should try our best to handle the current problems as far as possible and at the same time guide people to understand the duality and long-term process of the problems. In particular, we should guide people to remain committed to liberating and developing productive forces. Basically, only through constantly liberating and developing productive forces can we secure the most fundamental and important material premise to realize this "dual mission." Departing from the center of liberating and developing productive forces, or departing from the CPC's devotion on the economy and exploring the fundamental principles and directions for development, we not only make it impossible to talk about anything but mess things up instead. In a developing nation like ours, a developing country with a population of 1.3 billion to 1.5 billion, it is especially inadvisable to deal with such vital and strategic issues as such.

Third, we must realize that the great cause of modernization that we are now focusing on is in itself a "dual mission" never seen before in the history of the world. That is, we must continue to complete the traditional industrialization that has already been achieved in developed countries and meanwhile bring about industrialization through information technology so as to catch up with the new "great revolution" in modern science and technology that has been in the ascendant from the 1970s to the present. The resulting peculiar complexity is the dual historic challenge we face. First, we face challenges to advance the industries marked by big machines and electrification and realized by capitalism in the 200 years from the mid-18th century to the mid-20th century; second, we face challenges posed by the new technological revolution which is characterized by information technology, bio-engineering, new materials, new energy sources and so on. This new technological revolution was initiated by capitalism in the 1970s and is still unfolding. Therefore, we must hurry to catch up, shorten and eliminate the gap developed in at least a century or more in the past, and strive to complete industrialization. We also have to catch the tide of the new technological revolution and advance to a new level of modernization in the mid-21st century.

This means that the productive forces that China needs to liberate and develop in the first half of the 21st century cannot merely meet the same level of productivity as those of the "steel civilization" and "mechanical civilization" under the old mode of operation. Neither should China repeat the old mode of development by replacing labor with technology and capital. Instead, China should upgrade its industrial operation, equipment, and core technology to fully release innovation vitality to the level of IT-driven industrialization and ecological civilization. At the same time, it is also necessary to liberate entrepreneurial vitality on the foundation of a better configuration of capital, technology, and labor so as to create sustained and sufficient employment to support a populous nation.

Here I would like to stress again that the major "dual mission" decided by the most basic national conditions in contemporary China as mentioned above are unprecedented in terms of their breadth, depth and the impact on so many people's livelihood and development, never seen in the industrialization and modernization history of all previous powers or in the history of socialist countries in the world.

In short, the great cause and challenge require us to actively and voluntarily participate in economic globalization with Marxist courage and wisdom; and to have the Marxist insight and intelligence to respond to the challenges and risks that have emerged and may arise in the course of economic globalization. Only in this way will we be able to independently build socialism with Chinese characteristics and open up the strategic path of peaceful rise while staying connected with, rather than separated from, economic globalization.

Chapter 4

Duality of the Third Round of Economic Globalization

It is quite a surprise that after 40 years of economic globalization, the third round of economic globalization is seeing an astonishing reverse of this trend among some of the world's major powers. "Where economic globalization is heading to" has become a hot topic worldwide. How did this happen? Where is the crux of the problem? Can we therefore totally deny economic globalization? This is the focus of this chapter.

1. A historic debate on the future of economic globalization

The question of "where economic globalization is heading" comes into focus because the global community has a huge ongoing debate on the pros and cons of economic globalization. This phenomenon can also be regarded as a kind of contemporary form of the "Contention of Hundreds of Schools of Thoughts" that took place during the Spring and Autumn and the Warring States periods (770-221 BC) in ancient China.

Chinese history shows that any transition to a new chapter is marked by a historic debate among various schools of thoughts. It seems to be the same with world history. In the advent of the first and the second round of economic globalization, there had been such historic debates engaging various parties. Marx, Engels and Lenin all once participated in such debates, and history has substantiated their insightful observations. At the very beginning of the third round of economic globalization, a historic debate broke out around the 1980s, including large-scale demonstrations drawing tens of thousands of people protesting against economic globalization. China also saw heated discussion about whether or not to participate in economic globalization. However, the latest development is that a major debate on the future of economic globalization is now taking place all over the world.

Let's just look at the recent 2016 US presidential election and the 2017 French presidential election, as well as other referendums, debates and other incidents in Europe. These major events of 2016 and 2017 are now history yet how much attention have they drawn from the public? While the big news was certainly who would be the president-elect during the campaign, the political sentiment and political orientation expressed by the politicians and voters in those countries drew even greater concern. These emotions and tendencies have turned into "trend of thoughts." The most remarkable of these is the unprecedented trend of anti-globalization.

Originally, the various policies proposed by the two candidates in the US presidential election were all related to domestic issues, on which we need not to comment. However, a strong signal conveyed by the President-elect Trump during his campaign is: "The United States is shifting its direction." This signal has been received by all countries in the world, especially allies of the United States, and the response has never been stronger. In particular, the world has noticed that Trump's policy proposals are not only about the US domestic issues, but also about a major global issue: Where is economic globalization heading?

The United States has been long safeguarding its world dominance through economic globalization, which can be regarded as a fundamental national policy. The essence of economic globalization is trade liberalization. Many scholars have noticed that the changes in US national policy are mostly related to trade liberalization. Of course, many scholars have also noticed that such changes did not begin with Trump. After the global financial crisis triggered by the US subprime mortgage crisis in 2008, the economies of many countries fell into sustained downturn and sluggish recovery. Many countries have turned their attention toward regional cooperation or bilateral cooperation to protect local economies. In particular, the United States has taken more than 600 trade protection measures from 2008 to 2016, and launched 90 measures in 2016 alone, that is, a measure to protect its economy was introduced every four days. Therefore, the Trump phenomenon in the United States is not occasional but a collective manifesto of the worries, fears and distaste of trade liberalization that have existed in the nation for a long time.

In addition to the United States, Europe has also seen this phenomenon. After the sovereign debt crisis, European countries are facing a similar dilemma: the balance between the interests of European integration and the interests of their individual countries. The massive influx of refugees from the Middle East has further exacerbated the challenge and polarization in Europe. The Brexit referendum and the Italian referendum reflected the shift in public opinion. Although deglobalization will not happen immediately in Europe, the impact of this trend of thought has become noticeable. The 2017 French presidential election once again caught the eye of the world. Of the 11 candidates, Macron and Le Pen advanced to the runoff vote by winning 24.01% and 21.3% of the votes, respectively. On the issue of economic globalization, Macron supported free trade. Le Pen voiced her intention to reject international trade agreements, abolish the euro and benefit French enterprises through intelligent protectionism if taking office; and she even raised the possibility of holding a referendum on France's EU membership. Macron's final victory in this election has temporarily put Europe and the world at ease. However, the enormous influence that Le Pen and her populism and anti-globalization have exerted in France has indeed drawn the attention of the international community.

The grand debate that broke out in the United States and Europe touched upon all aspects of their domestic and foreign policies. However, the focus has always been on the issue of economic globalization and national security associated with this issue.

2. How to evaluate the third round of economic globalization that is designed and led by the United States

As mentioned previously, the third round of economic globalization was led by the developed Western countries and guided by the United States, of which the pros and cons have caused extensive discussions. This has also led to the question about the future of economic globalization. This historic debate on this issue involves two basic questions: first, how to evaluate the third round of economic globalization that has taken place in the past 40 years; second, how to assess the future of this round of economic globalization. Here, let us first discuss the first basic question, that is, how to evaluate the third round of economic globalization that is designed and led by the United States.

For the third round of economic globalization, we can make a duality analysis. On the one hand, economic globalization, as a mode of economic operation, is an objective requirement and an inevitable result when socialized production progresses to a certain stage. On the other hand, in general, economic globalization operates under the condition that the United States, as the sole superpower, designs, dominates, and profits hugely from it. Therefore, it is a "double-edged sword" for developing countries and poses same duality to developed countries.

In World War II, unlike the Soviet Union, European countries and China, the United States basically kept its territory free from war. Under the post-war protracted Cold War between the United States and the Soviet Union, the United States established its leadership through the implementation of the "Marshall Plan" to aid Europe's recovery. After the Soviet Union collapsed and the bipolarity ended, the United States became the only superpower. This made the United States a "leader" in the new round of economic globalization after World War II, with advantages that no other country had. Not to mention military superiority, but on economic superiority alone, the US had the following advantages: First, the production force especially created by the revolutionary new science and technology in the United States after the war brought together a group of high-tech industries, represented by information technology, and the transformed traditional industries (including automobile and steel). Second, in the "Bretton Woods system" established in the US after the war and the subsequent monetary system reform, the United States established the US dollar's de facto world currency status. Third, the United States has about US$24 trillion of financial assets. Fourth, the United States is in fact the big boss of major international financial organizations and has the power to dominate these organizations. Fifth, before the outbreak of the subprime mortgage crisis in 2008 and its impact on the international economic crisis, the US-led G7 has long been the enactor of the "game rules" for the international economy. Sixth, the United States has multinational financial institutions and their information networks cover the whole world. Seventh, the United States constantly develops increasingly sophisticated financial derivatives (futures, etc.) to attract and dominate investment and various essential resources in other countries. Eighth, the United States also has a full range of young professionals from many countries who are armed with the latest "financial engineering."

To sum up, the US influence on the third round of economic globalization comes from its comprehensive national strength, especially its economic strength. At the beginning of this round of economic globalization, the US GDP accounted for 25% of the world's total (1988) and rose to 27% in 1996; its share of the world trade also increased from 12% to 14% over the same period. Since 1992, the United States has regained its position as the world's largest and the most competitive exporter. In sharp contrast, Japan, the world's second-largest economy after its recovery from World War II throughout the 1980s and early 1990s, made a massive investment in the United States only resulting in a loss of US$700 billion (roughly equivalent to Japan's total trade surplus with the United States in the 1980s.) At the same time, as a result of the burst bubble economy, Japan's economic losses amount to US$10 trillion; coupled with the mistakes in the technical route of certain high-tech industries, the result was a serious recession lasting unprecedentedly long after the war. In short, its economic strength and control over the global economy have made US a "leader" in the third round of economic globalization in the past 40 years.

Then, how do we evaluate this round of economic globalization?

First, this round of economic globalization occurred at a time when the Cold War had ended, international relations, in particular East-West and the North-South relations, experienced great changes, and there emerged a global trend toward peace and development. These enormous changes expanded the global market's reach and scope in an unprecedented manner, and paved the way for the rapid growth of the global economy. The emergence of multinational companies and their quick growth also accelerated the integration of the global market. While economic globalization expanded the world market, it also gave impetus to economic reforms, economic restructuring, and technological innovations in various countries. A notable example of the trend is the development of international finance and financial innovations which, in turn, helped to expedite the rapid growth of the economy. Also connected to economic globalization is the flow of talent, including the rapid growth of entrepreneurs, which facilitated economic transition and development on a global and national basis. The heroes of today are no longer military commanders, or generals, but entrepreneurs like Bill Gates and Steve Jobs.

In the meantime, this round of economic globalization has brought about leapfrog development in some developing countries. In the tide of economic globalization, developing countries may either be marginalized or develop themselves by using global market expansion. In the course of this round of economic globalization, a group of developing countries in Southeast Asia, South Asia and Africa have taken advantage of the opportunity to promote trade liberalization through increased economic openness, wherein they have obtained capital, market, resources, advanced technology, management experience and other favorable conditions that were difficult to obtain in the past, and achieved leapfrog economic development. As Malaysian Deputy Prime Minister Abdullah Ahmad Madawi said, since the mid-1980s, a large influx of foreign direct investment and an open international trading environment have allowed our exports to grow. As a result, rapid industrialization and modernization in East Asian countries has been unprecedented.

November 3, 2016. Meeting with former Pakistani Prime Minister Shaukat Aziz at the CIIDS

China is a typical example of a developing country. After China decided to implement the policy of opening to the outside world and participate in economic globalization, it also drew on and utilized foreign investment and advanced management experience in domestic reform.

At the beginning of reform and opening up (1979-1982), China attracted a total of US$1.166 billion of foreign direct investment. Since then, it has risen year by year and grew rapidly from the 1990s. The actual utilized foreign direct investment has remained the second largest in the world since 1993, ranked the first among developing countries. At the same time, economic globalization has facilitated foreign scientists and multinational corporations to come to China. China thus is able to establish its own high-tech industries and to innovate by seizing and utilizing the opportunities brought about by the new technological revolution. In particular, China has implemented an all-round open policy of "bringing in" and "going out" to join the WTO, giving full play to the comparative advantages of Chinese products, expanding overseas markets and encouraging Chinese enterprises to actively participate in international competitions in a broader area. That is to say, in developing socialism with Chinese characteristics, China has seized the opportunity provided by economic globalization and achieved leapfrog development in its economy.

In short, to make an objective assessment of the third round of economic globalization that originated in the 1970s, we must recognize its contribution to the growth of the world economy and the economic take-off of developing countries. Of course, we must also recognize that the reason why developing countries, especially China, can achieve leapfrog development is related not only to economic globalization but also to the correct corresponding policies adopted by these countries in the process of economic globalization.

On the other hand, the issue is that the third round of economic globalization does have problems that cannot be underestimated. The first is the fundamental pursuit of the United States to design and lead economic globalization – to safeguard its global dominance as the sole superpower. It is clear this has never changed during or after the Cold

April 15, 2014. Meeting with then Indonesian President Susilo Bambang Yudhoyono during his visit to Indonesia

War. And this is exactly the fundamental conflict that the third round of economic globalization cannot overcome – the conflict between the interests of the United States and the rest of the world. This situation has led to the fact that the United States strives to promote economic globalization that marked by investment and trade liberalization when the expansion of the global market is in the interest of the United States. When its interests are hit hard in the competitive world market, the United States will do everything possible to suppress the economies that pose a threat to it even at the expense of the principles of cross-border investment and free trade that should be the base of economic globalization. This is why bitter conflicts of interest have repeatedly occurred between the United States and its political allies, including Japan, and countries in Europe and Southeast Asian in the 40 years of economic globalization. If taking into consideration the latest US move today, we can see that the United States, the "leader" of economic globalization, is talking about giving up and acting against globalization. What is reflected here is the enormous contradiction between the extensive outreach on the part of the US and the limitation of its own strength and the huge contradiction between seeking hegemony and the growing trend toward multipolarity and economic globalization. This is exactly the historical contradiction that cannot be overcome.

This round of US-led economic globalization still has another fundamental conflict that cannot be resolved. It is the conflict between its own capital and its own people. As the world's leading superpower, the United States is unmatched by other countries in economy, science and technology, and military. We can say that the United States escorts its economic hegemony and expansion with a superior military force. Such a strategy has continued to this day and is intensifying. But in the meantime, the US is exhausted by its domestic conflicts. Aren't the current events a good indicator? We can see that profit-driven capital in the United States has led to a flood of out-of-control financial derivatives, which has led to a massive bubble in the fictitious economy caused by the speculative economy. As a result, commercial goods have become heavily dependent on import, resulting in trade deficits; a hollowed domestic economy affects people's employment, resulting in low savings rates, underinvestment, rising labor costs and declining productivity; and government fiscal deficits or tax increases that cause social unrest, resulting in a polarized society and intensified social conflicts. And the huge national debt is an enormous bubble itself! These serious conflicts and problems in US society are the deepest roots of a series of global concerns or such world-class scandals as the subprime mortgage crisis, the shutdown of the government, the rise of populism, and the scandalous presidential election.

As some international experts of political science put it, "The Trump phenomenon will continue even if President Trump resigns tomorrow." That said, the Trump phenomenon is not so much Trump's personal character and trait as the "structural elements" of the United States. First, the wealth distribution in the United States is seriously unbalanced. The richest 1% of Americans have an average annual income of US$1.3 million. Among them, those whose wealth mainly comes from financial products, especially hedge funds, have higher incomes than those who gain profits in real economy. According to a survey conducted by the Massachusetts Institute of Technology, in the 40 years from 1973 to 2013, the actual average income of the middle class and the working class rose by only 4%, despite an 80% increase in labor productivity in the United States. Therefore, the American middle class and the working class have reason to be angry about this "inequity." Second, the United States sees serious political corruption. American politics has been manipulated by Wall Street financiers. In the past 27 years, more than half of the political donations from financial sectors, especially over 70% from hedge fund managers, have flown into politicians' pockets. In addition, 42% of the House Representatives and 50% of the Senators have enacted bills and worked out budgets for the benefit of interest groups during their tenure. After leaving office, they become lobbyists. Working as a lobbyist, the annual income is two or three times more than that of one's earnings in office. In this way, the political environment in which parliamentarians and entrepreneurs collude with each other is also an important reason why the society has decreasing trust in the "elite." Third, the US ethnic structure is changing. In the last seven years, more than half of all newborns in the United States are not white. By 2024, more than half of the population under the age of 20 are expected to be non-white; by 2042, more than half of the national population will be non-white. This in turn has greatly exacerbated the fears of immigration and intensified racism among the whites; it is also the reason why more than 60% of white voters in this presidential election supported Trump. It is fair to say that these serious "structural elements" are the reality of the

"Trump phenomenon."[1]

To sum up, the third round of economic globalization led by the United States has made a great contribution to the development of the world economy, but its role is limited as a result of conflicting problems that are difficult to overcome. This is the "duality" of this round of economic globalization.

3. Is China the cause of "American problems" in the context of economic globalization?

Before Trump took office, while implementing his "Asia-Pacific rebalancing" strategy, President Barack Obama claimed that China was catching up with the US by "riding its tailwind," and creating domestic employment problems in the United States and bilateral trade issues. Trump amplified this argument with added accusations and repeatedly threatened to initiate a trade war with China during his election campaign. In his first State of the Union Address not long ago, Trump even openly called China and Russia "revisionist powers," who were accountable for US issues. It can therefore be seen that blaming China for the "US problems" has become the "consensus" of US authorities, their think tanks and many of the elite.

Here, I would like to first answer some arguments put forward by Trump and his team.

Steve Bannon, Trump's campaign chief strategist, put it this way: "I am an economic nationalist. Globalization supporters (Asians, mainly Chinese) have destroyed the American working class and created a mid-

[1] *Reference News*, April 11, 2017.

dle class in Asia." (Bannon claimed that the Republicans represented by Donald Trump will stay in power for 50 years, but he himself stepped down in 50 days; and now he has openly turned against Trump.)

Of course, it is an undeniable fact that the 40-year economic globalization has turned into an increasing cost for US hegemony. But this is exactly its own making.

Think about this. Is the refugee problem caused by Asians or the Chinese? Is Middle East turmoil created by Asians or the Chinese? Is the Mexican immigration problem produced by Asians or the Chinese? Is it fair to place the blame for globalization, on Asians, or on the Chinese people? As for the "hollowing out" of the real economy and unemployment in the United States, is there any cause other than the various "strategies" adopted by major US financial groups in their pursuit of excessive profits?

It is in this context that populism is on the rise and utilized by the ruling power in the United States. This is the essence of these problems.

With further analyses of the current situation, we can say that the problems now attributed to economic globalization by the United States and some Western countries are in fact created under two conditions: First, economic globalization and advanced productive forces including the United States; second, the aggravated wealth disparity caused by capitalist groups of the United States and some Western countries in pursuit of profit without regard to their respective country's employment and people's livelihood. This is what many visionary people in the international community have pointed out – in the face of rising inequality, subversion is the daunting reaction as it turns its back on economic globalization and technological innovation.

We can make it more explicit with further explanations. After the Cold War ended, the victorious United States assumed the "end of history" had arrived and developed an attitude of superiority, exporting its values and political models everywhere and even deploying military forces for wars. What has been the result? US globalization has not only failed to truly dominate the world, but cost the nation several trillion dollars and 6,600 soldiers' lives in the two wars that aimed to "transform the Middle East," provoking terrorism and deep turmoil in various fields on top of a financial crisis. The real root cause here is, in plain language, the pride and arrogance of the American administration. Today, "grand pride" has shifted to the other extreme, a "grand reversal," that is, the "rogue action" to shake off the responsibility as a major power.

In short, the trend of anti-globalization has a long history and complex root causes.

As for China's actions in this third round of economic globalization, following are the facts:

1. After the fall of the Soviet Union, China did not follow the "end of history" thesis.

2. China withstood the great test after its accession to the WTO under harsh conditions.

3. China participated in economic globalization, without being fully integrated but adhering to independence and peaceful rise.

4. In domestic governance, instead of aggravating the polarization between the rich and the poor, China upholds common prosperity, including making major progress in poverty alleviation, in a productivity-centered process.

5. The result is that as the United States declines, China has become the world's second-largest economy (GDP).

The historical fact is that China also had some doubts about economic globalization and its accession to the World Trade Organization. However, the leadership of the CPC believed that participating in economic globalization was a historical trend and process. To develop its economy, China must dare to swim in the seas of the vast world markets. In the course of marching toward the world market, China has encountered ebb and flow but learned to swim by swimming. This is a correct strategy. Therefore, China has achieved rapid development on its own, not at the expense of the United States.

At the same time, it should be pointed out that it is only a matter of course that China has benefited from economic globalization through its normal economic and trade activities. How much has China, when opening up a domestic market of 1.3 billion people, brought to the world economies, including the United States? How much has China's rapid economic growth boosted global economic stability and growth? Therefore, China is a beneficiary and even more so a contributor to economic globalization. It is totally unreasonable to blame China for the economic and domestic problems in the United States.

Dealing with major issues like economic globalization, it is not a terrible thing for participants to have such problems in their own development. What is terrible is that participants, especially the leaders, cannot face the problems but try to find a scapegoat, which will not help solve the problem. To face the opportunities and challenges brought about by economic globalization and to make the right choices, we can only make full use of all opportunities, cooperate with each other in coping with all challenges and guide economic globalization in the right direction.

4. Ushering in economic globalization in a multi-polar world

Through the review and analysis of the third round of economic globalization, we can see that the problems that have emerged after 40 years are basically rooted in the guidance of the United States, in the fact that it promoted economic globalization for its own benefits. The crux of the problem is not whether we want economic globalization but what kind of economic globalization we want. As mentioned before, the third round of economic globalization has been going on for 40 years. Today, we have encountered two insurmountable issues: the conflict between the interests of US capital and the interests of the rest of the world; the conflict between the interests of US capital and the interests of its own people. As for those issues being "hard to overcome," it is because this round of economic globalization is designed and led by the United States or, in a broader sense, is dominated by the Western developed countries, wherein the interests of the United States or the US-led capital of the Western developed countries have played a major role. But if we look beyond the United States and the Western countries, then this "insurmountable" problem may turn out to be "not insurmountable."

As history shows us, during the 71 years since World War II ended, the world has seen several major changes, among which is the fall of the Soviet Union that ended the Cold War. Deng Xiaoping once expected the world to move toward "multi-polarization" from then on and the subsequent development actually validated this trend. However, the world is still basically one of "multiple big powers with one superpower," with the United States being the only superpower. For the United States, it could have been a historic opportunity. However, instead of drawing lessons from the Soviet Union, it was too eager to act as a "global hegemonist" and the "world police officer." In particular, starting with the September 11 terrorist attacks, the US became engaged in several wars in the Middle East. In the meantime, the subprime mortgage crisis took place in 2008, which in turn triggered the sovereign debt crisis in Europe. As a result, the world economy went into decline. Moreover, the combined factors of war expenditure and economic crisis have gradually aggravated the social conflicts within the United States. Against these multiple changes, Trump won the election with the slogan "America First" and "Make America Great Again." This, in turn, intensifies the conflicts with greater uncertainty, internally and externally. In addition, the increasing role of regional organizations such as the EU, ASEAN and the African Union, especially the rise of emerging powers such as China, Russia, India and South Africa, as well as the coming into being of the SCO and BRIC organizations, all foreshadow a major change in the world structure. Isn't this change signaling that the multipolar world structure Deng Xiaoping envisioned is gradually taking shape?

So, the actual situation is that such a great change in the world pattern has not only shown prominence but also exerted impact in the global economic governance. The role of the G20 is a good example. After the US subprime mortgage crisis and the European sovereign debt crisis, the G20 ascended the historical arena as an important new platform in global governance after the G7 had shown its limitations in this respect. G20 or the Group of Twenty is an international economic cooperation forum. It was originally proposed by the finance ministers of the seven industrialized countries including the United States to prevent similar recurrence of the Asian financial turmoil in 1998. Proposed in June 1999 in Cologne, Germany, it was then established on September 25 in Washington. G8 finance ministers announced the establishment of the G20 as a mechanism that was part of the informal dialogue within the framework of the Bretton Woods institutions attended by the finance ministers or central bank governors. Since the global financial crisis triggered by the US subprime mortgage crisis in 2008 made the financial system a global issue, the G20 has turned into a summit platform and actually replaced the previous G8 summit and the Group of 20 Finance Ministers Meeting. G20 members are China, the United States, Japan, Germany,

France, Britain, Italy, Canada, Russia, the European Union, Australia, South Africa, Argentina, Brazil, India, Indonesia, Mexico, Saudi Arabia, Turkey and South Korea. The gross national product of these countries amounts to about 85% of the world's total and their population adds up to nearly two-thirds of the world's total. Therefore, we should faithfully admit that the establishment of the G20 summit has brought new impetus and new opportunities for the international community to work together to cope with economic crises and promote reform of the global governance mechanism. The establishment of this platform marked a major shift from "Western governance" to "joint governance of Western and non-Western countries." The biggest difference between the G20 summit and the G7 or G8 summit is that the latter embodies the world's political structure of "multiple big powers with one superpower" in global economic governance, while the former represents a "multipolar" world political structure in global economic governance.

In short, the "multipolar" world structure envisioned by Deng Xiaoping is gradually taking shape. The G20 summit is only a manifestation of this profound change.

In this way, aren't there two types of "economic globalization"? One is the economic globalization dominated by the developed Western countries led by the United States and the other is economic globalization in a multi-polar world (including the United States and the developed Western countries). In other words, history is signaling the coming of economic globalization in a multi-polar world.

Here, we would like to share two "formulas" (Chinese experience):

The first one is "to independently pursue modernization with national characteristics in the process of participating in economic globalization."

The second is "to expand and deepen the converging point of the interests of all parties and to establish and develop communities of common interest among different countries and regions in all fields and at all levels."

October 12, 2015. The author and Indonesia's fifth president Megawati Sukarnoputri (second, left), eldest daughter of the first president of Indonesia Sukarno, presenting author's inscription for the Sukarno Home, or the Indonesia-China Cooperation Center in Shenzhen

We believe that the Chinese experience validates this orientation, which is needed and can be adopted in global development.

We expect such an orientation to win growing recognition and consensus within the international community.

Such an orientation, in the final analysis, is what President Xi Jinping calls "a global community of shared future" or, as he has repeatedly pointed out, "community of shared interests" and "community of shared future." If well executed, the notion with a series of relevant guidelines may make it possible to overcome the drawbacks of American-style globalization and prevent all kinds of isolationism.

Many people in the world now advocate China should fill in as the "leader" of economic globalization, a position vacated by the United States. They accept China's vision and we are grateful for their goodwill toward China. However, China is still a developing country which has not completed its modernization. Especially with a population of more than 1.3 billion, China has problems and challenges unimaginable to other countries. It is a hard truth without any doubt.

Of course, we must also make it clear that we, together with other countries in the world, are facing many challenges that are already big enough, namely, terrorism, nuclear proliferation, climate change, energy security, food and water safety, poverty alleviation, and financial crisis. All of these challenges are global in nature and have a direct bearing on the vital interests of hundreds of millions of people and can only be effectively addressed through expanding cooperation among nations and

October 2009. Meeting with former US Vice President Al Gore (second, left) and Chair of the Board of Trustees of the Brookings Institution John L. Thornton (first, left) during the First US-China Strategic Forum on Clean Energy Cooperation

responsible governance.

Another issue that needs to be highlighted is that Western countries like to sell their values and political systems. They even use their standards as a weapon to remediate and subvert non-Western countries, as demonstrated by the US action of "transforming the Middle East." We think it is about the right time now to solemnly affirm that only the people of a nation have the right to choose the development path and system deemed suitable to that nation, not to be judged according to Western values and political systems. As an old Chinese saying goes: "Only the wearer of the shoes knows whether they fit or not."

Presented before us is a major issue of principle: Economic globalization under the leadership of the United States can no longer meet the demand of the new situation in the new stage of history. In other words, we need to plan a new framework. This is exactly what President Xi Jinping recently put forward at the G20 summit. In the most general terms, President Xi Jinping's stance is as follows: first, to remain committed to openness so as to increase the size of the global economic "pie"; second, to explore new impetus to the world economy through innovation; third, to achieve balanced global growth through inclusiveness; fourth, to improve global economic governance through joint actions.

This is the trend of the world going forward. The dual-nature development of the third round of economic globalization has today ushered in a new round of globalization, which is based on a multipolar world that revolves around a community of common interests and shared future (instead of the "strategic balance of major powers") and seeks "peace and development" (as opposed to "domination" or "hegemony.")

Chapter 5

"Global Community of Shared Future" Based on "Common Interests" and "Community of Shared Interests" and the International Relations Theory of the New Era

In the preceding chapters, we have discussed China's new path for peaceful development during reform and opening up and the duality of the third round of economic globalization, noting that we are embracing economic globalization in a multi-polar world. How could China embark on the path of peaceful rise in economic globalization? What is the foundation for economic globalization in a multi-polar world? The answer to these two interrelated questions lies in a "community of shared future" based on "common interests" and "community of shared interests" which we have discussed in Section III, Chapter 1 and in Section IV, Chapter 4. What underpins the discussions here is a brand new theory of international relations that is adapted to the needs of the new era.

1. The strategic blueprint for international relations in an era of peace and development

As we have discussed, China is not alone on the path of peaceful rise today. Many other developing countries have taken the same path. Fundamentally, it is because economic globalization in an era of peace and development and the global markets have made countries a closely-knit community with common and shared interests. At the invitation of the 21st Century Council[1], I gave a keynote speech at its Paris Forum on October 26, 2011, calling for "expanding common interests and building a community of shared interests." Unanimously accepted, it was written into the forum's declaration and submitted to the G20 Summit as the "guiding concept of the 21st Century Council."

I called, in my keynote speech, for "expanding common interests and building a community of shared interests." This strategic blueprint was drawn based upon China's strategies and goals of development for the second decade of the 21st century. China has been striving to accelerate the transformation of the economic development pattern, guarantee and improve people's lives, boost steady economic growth, promote social

---

[1] Established in 2011, the 21st Century Council aims to press G20 countries to play a role in the global governance. The Council sees the G20 as a result of the changing global geopolitics and an effective mechanism dealing with current challenges. Thus, the Council calls itself "the Shadow G20." Core members include former French President Nicolas Sarkozy, former German Chancellor Gerhard Schröder, former British Prime Minister Gordon Brown, former Brazilian President Fernando Henrique Cardoso, former Spanish Prime Minister Felipe González Márquez, former Mexican President Ernesto Zedillo, former Pakistani Prime Minister Shaukat Aziz, former Secretary of the US Treasury Lawrence Summers, former Director-General of the WTO Pascal Lamy, Nobel Laureate in economics Joseph E. Stigllitz, and Nobel Laureate in chemistry Ahmed Zewail. The 21st Century Council invited Zheng Bijian as its "founding director" and to the summit forum held in Paris in late October 2011.

harmony and stability, and build a moderately prosperous society. Accordingly, China has entered a period in which its growth will be driven by domestic rather than external demand; and the focus of opening up is shifted from export and foreign capital absorption to the equal emphasis on export and import and on foreign capital absorption and investment overseas. Also, industrial restructuring and upgrading of consumption structure are accelerated; and China strives to turn from a lower middle-income country to an upper middle-income one. Therefore, China will focus more on domestic development and improved quality and spiritual pursuits, so that Chinese society remains a stable and harmonious one full of vitality and the Chinese nation realizes a peaceful rise and rejuvenation of the Chinese civilization. Undoubtedly, such a China will be a place with huge market demand and more opportunities for the entire world. I also noted that in the first decade of the 21st century, China steadily followed the path of peaceful rise and became an important part of world development, and there were growing interests shared between China and the rest of the world . Then in the second decade of the 21st century, China will unremittingly follow the path of peaceful rise and play a more important role in the world, to build shared interests with other countries in a more systematic and sustainable manner. This fundamentally defines the relationship between China and the rest of the world in the coming decade and after.

Of course, China has built its vision of peaceful rise upon the general trend in the world. I talked about my predictions on the world situation in my speech.

First of all, in economic globalization in a multipolar world, countries are getting more interconnected and interdependent.

Second, major-country relations are experiencing significant changes and the trend of competition and cooperation is becoming more prominent. The G20 summits have shown major countries need to cooperate for development and seek advantage in competition. It is imperative to keep competition within reasonable limits and expand cooperation.

Third, large developing countries, including China, are generally gaining momentum in peaceful rise. The coming decade is critical to their development and rise. The BRICS Summit held in Sanya in April 2011 further demonstrated the unstoppable consciousness and momentum of the peaceful rise of emerging powers.

Fourth, the international financial crisis has boosted a great transformation of social productivity around the globe. A new "green, low-carbon and sustainable" technological and industrial revolution is blooming.

Fifth, the profound impacts of the international financial crisis still exist and the world's economic recovery faces uncertainties. In the post-crisis times, global security issues such as climate, energy, resources, food, and finance have become even more prominent. The issue of global governance has been urgently put on the agenda.

Sixth, major countries will see substantial changes in their economic development modes. Accordingly, the relative status and interest relations of major countries will experience changes.

Seventh, in a complicated world, what is good and positive grows alongside with what is bad and negative. Severe turbulence or geopolitical conflicts and the danger of traditional warfare still exist. Turbulent situations in West Asia and North Africa have taught people to remain calm but cautious. While democracy is the general trend in the world, it should not be externally imposed at the cost of peace. Rather, the people of a country should have the right to choose the path befitting them, the right way in which human rights, democracy and rule of law may be ensured.

Eighth, no matter how the world changes, international relations will be dominated by sovereign states for a long time to come. As the Sanya Declaration of the BRICS Leaders Meeting stated, "We maintain that the independence, sovereignty, unity and territorial integrity of each nation should be respected."

And lastly, on the whole, China and the rest of the world will see opportunities and challenges intertwined while opportunities are greater than challenges. We are confident of a peaceful development of China in the coming decade and we will not waver, despite various incidents or crises.

The above are the development trends of the world that I have observed for now and for the next decade.

Based on my analysis of China's development strategies and goals for the second decade of the 21st century and on my prediction about the trends in the world's development, I also proposed in my speech to expand common interests and to build a community of shared interests between China and the EU.

First of all, let's have a look at the relationship between China and the EU. Since the outbreak of the financial crisis in 2008, particularly since 2010, China and the EU have both been confronted with enormous internal challenges that are much greater than threats from the outside.

Development and stability remain the most urgent and pressing issues for China. The problems that warrant immediate attention include inflation expectations, exchange market pressures, widening income gap and real estate bubbles. In the long run, China has to deal with economic restructuring, lagging technology and education, and social governance in urgent need of being strengthened and optimized.

The biggest challenge for the EU lies in its internal adjustments and reform rather than challenges from the outside world. The EU's top priority is to balance budgets, clear off debts, return to positive growth, and improve its international competitiveness.

To address their respective challenges, both China and the EU need a stable external environment, a progressive reform of the international regime, and a mild method of global governance. This is where their common interests lie. The promotion of common interests and the building of a community of shared interests will have a solid foundation, when both China and the EU deem maintaining each other's stability and the stability of the international order the top priority for their common interests.

Secondly, China is a major trade partner of the EU. The two economies are highly interdependent. Job opportunities can be created in EU countries by reducing and even removing trade and investment barriers and encouraging the investment of Chinese enterprises. Likewise, European companies will also find ample investment opportunities in China. In addition, strengthening consultation on the future global monetary system and financial regulatory mechanisms and pushing forward relevant reforms will play an important role in the balanced development of the world economy. This is also an interest shared between China and the EU.

Thirdly, China and Europe see common interests in many other areas. Climate and energy are areas with best potential for cooperation. China is one of the largest energy consumers, crude oil importers, and carbon emitters in the world today. Europe is highly dependent on imported energy as well. By 2030 its energy dependence will reach 70%. Sino-European cooperation in clean energy will boost the economic development and scientific and technological innovation in both China and Europe. Our common interests lie in many other areas, including network security, space safety, and security at sea, all of which are important for the well-being of humanity. Thus, such areas should be seen as "common areas." It is highly necessary to establish common rules and operational modes recognized by all the countries concerned.

Fourthly, China and the EU have shared interests in non-traditional security issues, in maintaining stability in the Middle East, Central Asia and South Asia, and in counter-terrorism.

Fifthly, to build a community of shared interests means each must exercise caution when responding to the other's sensitive issues. Efforts are required to maintain stability along the Taiwan Strait and secure the peaceful development of cross-strait relations. China and the EU have no direct strategic divergence in this issue. However, there are still issues of implications. For instance, the EU refuses to lift the ban on the sale of weapons to China, reportedly for reasons refuses to to Taiwan. In contrast, EU countries are selling weapons to Taiwan.

Sixthly, it is a long and painstaking process for China and the EU to build a community of shared interests, during which disputes and divergences may occur. However, the factors and driving forces for enhanced Sino-EU relations in the coming decade remain. Thus, we need to bear in mind the importance of expanding common interests and building a community of shared interests, and discover new engines for the development of bilateral and multilateral relations in order to achieve mutual benefits and win-win results.

Seventhly, it is noteworthy that China's call for expanding "common interests" and building a "community of shared interests" is a multi-faceted strategic blueprint. It is never something exclusive. The blueprint is designed for China and the EU, as well as for China and the US, other Asian countries, Africa, and Latin America. In short, China aims, by integrating the Chinese people's interests with those of the other peoples in the world, to expand common interests and build communities of shared interests with other countries and regions in different areas and on various levels, so as to promote the common interests of humanity and share the achievements of human civilizations.

Finally, I want to emphasize once again that "expanding common interests" and "establishing and developing communities of shared interests in different fields and on different levels with various countries and regions" has been a major policy of the Communist Party of China

November 2, 2015. Meeting with former Singaporean Prime Minister Goh Chok Tong at the Second Understanding China Conference

and the Chinese Government. President Hu Jintao and Premier Wen Jiabao had reiterated this on many international occasions. China made this stance clear in the CPC Central Committee's suggestion on the 12th Five-Year Plan and in the white paper *China's Peaceful Development Road* published on September 6 this year.

As I have mentioned, some EU countries are currently mired in debt. It is a challenge, and at the same time, a great chance for the in-depth integration of the EU and for China and the EU to find more common interests. As history has shown, the EU becomes more integrated after each crisis. We hope that it is not an exception this time. China and the EU will pull together in times of trouble, as the two have common interests.

My speech at the 21st Century Council's Paris Forum not only explained the basic reasons for China's peaceful rise, but also further elaborated the path of peaceful rise. I hope and firmly believe that this will be increasingly accepted by the international community.

2. Will China and the US find common interests and build a community of shared interests?

Sino-US relations are the top priority of China's diplomacy. Politicians and strategists from many countries have attached importance to Sino-US relations as well. Then, can China and the US find common interests and build a community of shared interests? As early as on November 10, 1989 when Deng Xiaoping had a meeting with Kissinger, Deng gave his opinion on the issue, "The times when interstate relations were determined by the social system have long gone. Countries of different social systems can coexist peacefully, become friends and find their common interests. China and the US will definitely find their shared interests."[2]

I had a meeting with former US Secretary of State Dr. Kissinger in Beijing on June 26, 2011. We exchanged extensive ideas on how to expand common interests and build a community of shared interests between China and the US, in our five-and-half-hour talk.

I told Dr. Kissinger that our talk would focus on "two overall situations" and "how to expand common interests and build a community of shared interests between China and the US." The "two overall situations" referred to the domestic and international situation, particularly what China and the US were facing. I put "two overall situations" ahead of everything else, because I found new urgent problems to be solved both for China and the US at the very beginning of the second decade of the

---

[2] *Chronicle of Deng Xiaoping (1975-1997)*, Vol. II, Central Party Literature Press, 2004, Chinese edition, p. 1297.

21st century. Whether the two nations properly deal with those urgent problems, or whether the two have an appropriate understanding of their domestic and international situations, play a key role in the development of the two countries, in their relations, and in the situation in Asia-Pacific and even the world in the second decade of the 21st century.

October 19, 2011. Meeting with former US Secretary of State Henry Kissinger during his visit to New York

My talk with Dr. Kissinger mainly covered the following points.

1. Both China and the US need to focus on their domestic affairs when we deal with our domestic and international situations. That is one thing in common. To do this, we both need a stable external environment, a progressive reform of the international order, and mild global governance. We will see a broad and solid foundation for their "common interests" and "community of shared interests," once we make maintaining the other's stability and securing the stability of the international order the top common interests of China and the US.

2. The US leaders state that the US is unable to or does not intend

to subvert the Chinese government or contain China. We are willing to believe that this is said out of sincerity, instead of merely diplomatic parlance. In the meantime, China does not intend to challenge or subvert the US historically-built position in the world and Asia-Pacific. And the US should believe that this is said out of sincerity, instead of merely diplomatic parlance. So long as China and the US both are true in word and resolute in deed, we will see our common interests well secured in a long run in the 21st century.

3. At present, the US government's top priority is not security challenges. Instead, it needs urgently to deal with the severely challenging economic situation, including huge debts and unbalanced budget, unsteady economic growth, insufficient investment and persistently high unemployment, as well as people's wavering faith in the US dollar. Development and stability remain the most urgent issues to be dealt with by the Chinese government. The country is under pressure from inflation expectations and exchange rates. The income gap gets larger and the real estate industry is bubbling. In the long run, China has to deal with economic restructuring, lagging technology and education, and social governance which are in urgent need of being strengthened and optimized. Also, economic problems in China and the US impact the development of the other. Thus, macroeconomic policy conciliation and sectoral economic complementarities have been put on the agenda of our dialogue and interactions, as the most important part of our bilateral cooperation.

4. China and the US see much room for cooperation in issues concerning the Middle East, Central and South Asia. Stability in the Persian Gulf, Red Sea, Suez Canal and countries in those regions plays a critical role in the global petroleum supply, and contributes to the common interests of China and the US. It remains a long-term mission of both of us to fight hard against terrorist forces in those areas.

Of course, when addressing the aforementioned issues, we need to give full consideration of the complicated situations in the Middle East, and Central and South Asia. Historically and presently, external interventions have achieved little in those areas, which are complicated by racial, tribal and religious interests. Chronic regional turmoil inevitably has far-reaching negative impact on energy security, counter-terrorism, and non-proliferation of nuclear weapons around the globe.

5. China and the US have most shared and conflicting interests in security issues of East Asia (including Northeast and Southeast Asia). The key is to expand common interests and reduce conflicts. We can neither evade the issue, nor be disrupted by external and internal factors. China and the US have much to do to prevent any incident-triggered crises on the Korean Peninsula. The situation in Taiwan and across the Taiwan Strait needs to stay stable. But the Sino-US cooperation in this field is far from sufficient. Arms sales to Taiwan remains a highly sensitive issue for both China and the US, and should not be allowed to undermine comprehensive Sino-US cooperation. At present, maritime security in Asia remains the most delicate issue in Sino-US relations. The issue actually includes three smaller ones, namely territorial disputes in the East China Sea and South China Sea, freedom of navigation, and reconnaissance carried out by the US Air Force in Chinese coastal waters. The three issues must be treated discriminatingly and properly. Any conflict-exacerbating actions must be avoided, in case the issues get more complicated. This is the start point for China and the US to find common interests and build a community of shared interests in the region in question. China adopts an open and inclusive approach and a policy for friendly cooperation in East Asia, and welcomes the US and Russia to join the East Asia Summit.

6. Multilateral economic cooperation in the Asia-Pacific plays a significant role in building a Sino-US community of shared interests or what Dr. Kissinger called the "Pacific community." China has promoted

"open regionalism" within the 10+X framework, and welcomes US to join in the regional cooperation mechanism in East Asia. Similarly, the US should open the TPP to China. The APEC has helped the integration of regional interests. But the forum is more or less loosely organized. Thus, more Sino-US negotiations are needed. The two countries should, by cooperation in Asia-Pacific, have regional issues better settled and bilateral economic issues satisfactorily solved, such as exchange rate, trade, technology transfer, and investment.

7. China and the US will find even greater space for cooperation in global governance. The G20 was founded at the initiative of China and the US. Our two countries have more common interests in climate and energy issues than in other areas. As the largest energy consumers, crude oil importers, and carbon emitters, China and the US have more in common than difference, in terms of emission standard and energy supply and demand. Finance and currency are another field in which China and the US find more common interests. Changes in the US dollar exchange rate have a great impact on China; in turn, China as a major holder of the US Treasure securities plays a significant role in the fiscal balance of the US. Thus, the two countries should hold frequent negotiations for the global monetary system and financial regulation mechanism in future, and make joint efforts to promote those systems, with the least harm to the two countries' interests.

8. As in the fields of cyberspace, space, polar, and maritime security and security of other public space, China and the US seem to be more in competition than cooperation. Nonetheless, the two countries can have much cooperation in those areas. Hacking remains a potential threat to the interests of both countries. Thus, cyberspace security should be guaranteed both for China and the US. Space, polar, and maritime security is crucial to humanity's safety. Both countries should make unremitting efforts to establish common rules and operational modes recognized by

January 2011. Meeting with then US Ambassador to China Jon Huntsman Jr. (second, right) and Carla Anderson Hills (first, left), chair of the National Committee on US-China Relations, during the Second US-China Strategic Forum on Clean Energy Cooperation

the countries concerned.

9. It is highly probable that China and the US will cooperate in non-traditional security issues, such as safe utilization of nuclear energy, ecological crisis and environmental protection, disaster relief, anti-narcotics, epidemic prevention and control, anti-money laundering, and crackdown on human trafficking and international crime organizations. Along with more frequent population movement and closer economic ties between the two countries, non-traditional security issues of either side may have butterfly effects on the other. Therefore, the two need stronger cooperation through better information sharing, assistance, and joint efforts, in a more systematic manner. They will benefit from helping each other.

10. Neither should simply regard the other as a rival, in areas of de-

mocracy, freedom, human rights and systems. A simplified judgment of culture and systems in ideology and Cold War mentality not only severely impairs the building of wider common interests, but also fundamentally goes against the facts and the rule of social development.

At the end of my talk, I said that not all the aforementioned ten points were new. Quite a number of them had been touched upon in Sino-US dialogues and in practice. My "ten-point reflection" was a summary of the strategic issues China and the US would have to deal with in order to develop their strategic relations in the second decade of the 21st century. What underpins all the points is the need to promote common interests and build a community of shared interests.

Dr. Kissinger took notes while listening. He said he was deeply impressed and would like to have further discussions with me. He told me he had been engaged in balance of power all his life, but it seemed it would not work in the 21st century. He agreed with my proposal to expand common interests and build a community of shared interests.

Dr. Kissinger also stressed that even though he had been an advocate of "checks and balances of power" all his life, he believed that China and the US should cooperate at a higher level that should go beyond "checks and balances" between big countries. He thought my "ten-point reflection" on "common interests" and "a community of shared interests" was valuable in this regard.

Dr. Kissinger wrote to me on July 12, 2011, praising my "ten-point reflections" as penetrating, ingenious, and well reflecting our common aspirations. He said he appreciated the insight my team and I had shown when discussing the widespread and deep-rooted issues in China and the US in different regions and around the globe.

Nonetheless, Sino-US relations became more complicated, due to the US "Pivot to Asia" and "Rebalance to Asia" policies. On June 20, 2014 I met in Beijing former US National Security Advisor Stephan Hadley and answered his questions on our troubled bilateral relations.

I told Hadley that we could have a discussion starting from the questions he put forward and I had something to say on that:

First of all, China found the year of 2014 both "a year of new prospect" and "a year of frustration," because China had defined its new plans for domestic and foreign affairs in 2014, as decided at the 18th CPC National Congress in 2012 and at the Third Plenary Session of the 18th Central Committee of the CPC in 2013. China had to go through a major test by dealing with numerous difficult issues appropriately.

The year of 2014 and even the year of 2015 would be crucial to Sino-US relations. We needed to seize this soon-to-pass chance. China was positive about the prospect of Sino-US cooperation, with an insightful observation of the Sino-US relations; that was to say, "China and the US should eventually be on good terms," as Deng Xiaoping put it. This was fully in line with the fundamental interests of China and the US. I believed Chinese leadership had never changed their thinking on this.

June 20, 2014. Meeting with former US National Security Advisor Stephen Hadley at the CIIDS

March 2, 2014. A group photo of guests attending the Fourth Forum on US-China Relations

Secondly, it was something concrete, not fable, in regard to the significance, benefits, and feasibility of developing Sino-US relations. There were realistically three reasons for this. First, in general, neither China nor the US was willing to see intense confrontations or severe conflicts. Secondly, China and the US had huge shared interests, particularly in economic cooperation. It was clear to see. And thirdly, there were disruptive forces, of course. But they were not powerful enough or fully prepared. Thus, China and the US must be clear-minded, determined and take resolute action. Otherwise, our bilateral relations would be adversely affected.

Thirdly, we needed to have deeper, broader, and more pragmatic observation of the general situation of the world. We needed strategic insight, rather than short-sighted calculation. In the US, some argued for containment of China. I would like to know what resources there were to realize this goal. At sea, the US might check China, at best on half of the routes. On land, behind China was Siberia, Central Asia, Russia and Europe. Thus, it was impossible to contain or block China. It was best to have good Sino-US relations. Suppression and containment would not work.

Some in the US were worried about the good relations between China and Russia. I wanted to make it clear that a good Sino-Russian relationship need not jeopardize good Sino-US relations. Instead, they promoted each other. I believed that "to be on good terms with the US" was not crossed out on the agenda of China's leaders. It was superficial to think that Sino-Russian relations were contradictory to Sino-US relations.

Fourthly, what mattered most now for Sino-US relations was what happened in the West Pacific. The US Asia-Pacific strategy was built on the US-Japan military alliance, openly declared by the Obama Administration as the "cornerstone." The US was for lifting the ban on collective self-defense from Japan and for Japan's "nationalization" of the Diaoyu Islands.

November 2, 2015. Meeting with former First Deputy Prime Minister of Russia Oleg Soskovets

I think it is right to see things historically and dialectically. The US-Japan military alliance had a long and tortuous history. Truthfully, the US created the alliance, initially to control Japan and the Asia-Pacific; to check the Soviet Union during the Cold War, and to contain China now with "Pivot to Asia" policy. But the US is not powerful enough to check China all by itself. It needs Japan's help. Therefore, the US policy on Japan is turned from controlling Japan to supporting the latter "to regain its right of collective self-defense" and "nationalize" the Diaoyu Islands. Moreover, like Japan, the US denies China's legitimate sovereignty.

I must make it clear to our American friends that it would not take too long to prove the attempt of containment of China and indulging Abe by relying on the US-Japan military alliance would, in turn, be a burden to the US and even a heavy one, politically, morally, and practically.

Fifthly, fundamentally, Asia-Pacific security is guaranteed via Sino-US cooperation and common development of countries in the Asia-Pacific, bearing in mind, historically, strategically, and morally, the idea that "the Pacific being amply vast" and building "a new pattern of relationship between major powers" between China and the US was the solution for Asia-Pacific security and for avoiding repeating the same mistake made in US-Russia relations during the Cold War.

Specifically, China and the US should make a joint effort to form common interests and a community of shared interests in three areas from now until 2020:

- Mutual benefits and win-win in economic cooperation;
- Peaceful cooperation in security issues; and
- Equal sharing of responsibility and rights in global governance.

Hadley appreciated what I had said, saying it was well thought-out and proved once again the significance of such a talk. He told me, it was very important to have faith in China in maintaining major-power relations in Asia and believed China wanted to be on good terms with the US. When he was in government, he talked about the significance of the US-Japan alliance, though he did not use the word "cornerstone." He had been firm in supporting a new type of relationship between China and the US, and also US relations with South Korea and Japan based on the treaties that they had reached. That was important. He emphasized he might be wrong, but that was what he had been firm on. He suggested we should work in four key areas, namely having strategic talks, including on trends and strategies; developing the principles for a new type of major-country relationships; creating two or three operable projects; and finding one or two bilateral disputes to settle.

At the end of the meeting Hadley hailed this talk as a good example of strategic talks. He said that it was good to put things on the table and have an in-depth talk, instead of reading from the prepared text, and that this was strategic communication in the true sense.

I must say, Sino-US relations will remain a key issue for the foreseeable future. Following Deng Xiaoping's strategic blueprint and giving full consideration to domestic and international situations, we need to dedicate ourselves to discovering our "common interests," expanding common interests, and building communities of shared interests in various areas and at various levels, in the complicated context of ever-changing international situations, so as to realize the sound development of Sino-US relations and maintain peace and common development around the globe.

3. Common interests and community of shared interests in the domestic and international context

International situations are complicated in the second decade of the 21st century. It is a challenge both for China and other major countries in the world to take the right path of development, appropriately deal with inter-state relations, expand common interests, and build a community of shared interests. And this is the issue I have been most thinking about and talking about with foreign friends in recent years.

Former US National Security Advisor Zbigniew Brzezinski paid a visit to the China Institute for Innovation & Development Strategy (CI-

June 29, 2013. Meeting with former US National Security Advisor Zbigniew Brzezinski at the CIIDS

IDS)[3] on June 29, 2013. As the institute's chairman, I held a long talk with Brzezinski on international situations and Sino-US relations. I had already had many previous meetings with Brzezinski. When we met in the US Center for Strategic and International Studies in 2011, Brzezinski commented on my ideas on "peaceful rise," "common interests" and "a community of shared interests," saying my theory of peaceful rise showed China's development path was different from any other major

---

[3] The China Institute for Innovation and Development Strategy (CIIDS) was founded in May 2010, with Mr. Zheng Bijian as its chairman. A group of renowned Chinese political figures, diplomats, military scholars, economists, public figures and academicians serve as senior advisors. Innovation and development are the main subjects of study of CIIDS, as they are interlinked and mutually reinforcing. The purpose of the study is to further explore China's path to peaceful rise or peaceful development. Specifically, CIIDS' studies concentrate on scientific and technological innovation, economic development, social governance, cultural advancement, and international strategy. It is engaged in academic exchanges and joint studies with relevant government departments, well-known universities, research institutions and enterprises at home and seeks cooperation and exchanges with relevant organizations abroad. The outcome of the studies will provide intellectual support and policy advice to the government in its decision-making process.

countries in history. Looking back into the last 100 years, conflicts between major powers led to World War I, World War II, and the Cold War. He noted what I proposed might help Sino-US relations avoid old mistakes.

In our 2013 talk, I said that the essential line of my thoughts for years has always been "major changes, new awakening." To put it more specifically, they are about major changes and a new awakening of China on peaceful rise, and those of the world in peaceful development. We may say, in the history of the world, it is a great course never seen before.

In the meantime, things are complicated. They are never single-sided. Duality has been another major feature of China's development in the past three decades or so. We have to deal with it calmly. When talking about "encirclement of China," I said that we must know the situation in Asia-Pacific now is not that before World War II, or World War I, let alone the late Qing period. China today is neither the Qing regime, nor Germany in World War I or Japan in World War II. It definitely will not work to go back to the old way of checking China by supporting Japan. In a word, encirclement of China is destined to fail. They must recognize and acknowledge the existence of a New East.

Brzezinski said he was deeply impressed and could observe the academic and political wisdom in what I had said. "You are a great theoretician who has original thoughts on the future of China and the world. And you have a global vision. You have insightful observation of social and economic development in China and the world. Your insight on cooperation and relationship between the world's two major countries is insightful." He went on to say that China and the US were not on the same wavelength at present. But they had the potential to take on more responsibility for the future of the world and other countries, making their relationship more historically significant. He expressed full agreement with my comment on the special responsibilities of the two countries.

In particular, both countries should have effective interaction on shared responsibility via closer cooperation. It would benefit both countries and the entire world."

In my talk with Japan's former speaker of the House of Representatives Yohei Kono[4] on October 17, 2014 in Beijing, we focused on "the world's situations in major changes."

What are those major changes? In my opinion, "the three regions" may have the greatest changes, namely, Eastern Europe under the shadow of the Ukraine Crisis, the Greater Middle East plagued with upheavals in Iraq, Syria, Israel and Palestine, and Iran, and the Asia Pacific disturbed by the US "Pivot to Asia" strategy. Different forces are involved in power struggles against the complicated situations in the three regions, having led to and continuing to generate radical changes. That's the first thing.

Secondly, in the three regions, any changes in the China-US-Russia Triangle will attract the most attention. However, this triangle is quite different from the China-US-Soviet Union Triangle in the Cold War, in terms of origin and connotation. Let's name it the New Triangle. One feature of this New Triangle is that Russia is approaching the East. Cornered by the US and other Western countries, Russia has no other choice. And China finds no reason to refuse Russia, in such a circumstance. Since Russia is forced to seek cooperation and win-win with China, why should we refuse? Naturally, the New Triangle emerged.

Thirdly, the two changes mentioned above have created a new inter-

---

[4] A renowned Japanese politician and an old friend of the Chinese people, Yohei Kono was once president of the Liberal Democratic Party (LDP), deputy prime minister of Japan, minister of foreign affairs, chief cabinet secretary, and speaker of the House of Representatives. When he was chief cabinet secretary, Yohei Kono made an official statement on the investigation of "comfort women" or forced prostitution on 4 August 1993, admitting for the first time that the Imperial Japanese Army coerced women in Asian countries to be military prostitutes during World War II.

August 20, 2015. Meeting with Yohei Kono, former speaker of the House of Representatives of Japan, at the CIIDS

national environment for China, i.e. "the two lines," one in the north and the other in the south. In the north, China is on good terms with Russia, Central Asia, other members of the Shanghai Cooperation Organization (SCO), and Europe. Premier Li Keqiang signed quite a number of cooperation agreements with Germany, Italy and Russia during his visit to Europe. Eurasia is a place with broad prospects. Is that a good thing? I think so. It is good both for China and the world. What is the benefit? We have seen an enlarged market and broader economic, cultural and scientific cooperation. Does that mean any threat of war? I do not think so. It is a positive, sound and healthy development. That is what has happened along the line in the north. Nonetheless, the northern line is plagued with problems, including terrorism and "three evil forces." What can we do? We must deal with them seriously and be ready for a protracted fight. Xinjiang of China is included here. Terrorists in Xinjiang maintain contact with terrorist forces in Central Asia and many other areas.

We have been clear about the situation and handled it step by step. On the whole, things are in control. What I would like to reiterate is that be it Sino-Russian relations or the SCO, it is a new type of open and non-exclusive partnership.

Fourthly, let's look at the southern line. It is something very troublesome, including Sino-Japanese and Sino-Vietnamese relations. And the root cause lies in the US "Pivot to Asia" strategy, based on the US-Japan military alliance as the "cornerstone" and on the attempt to lift the ban on "collective self-defense" in Japan. Some in Japan accuse China of provoking Japan. Did China provoke incidents on the Diaoyu Islands that have been Chinese territory from ancient times to the present? The Japanese government picked a fight by attempting to "nationalize" the islands. Did China provoke incidents in the South China Sea? In reality, China has advocated settling disputes via talks. But the fact is that the US has tried to control and check China via military power or even the US-Japan military alliance.

Fifthly, despite all what I said above, is the situation on the southern line hopeless? I don't think so. Personally, I think the situation will develop with "duality." On the one hand, some countries try to militarily check China, with the US-Japan military alliance at the core. On the other hand, economic, trade, financial, scientific and technological, and educational cooperation is needed. Sino-US economic cooperation is of a size unmatched in the world. Cooperation has taken shape and keeps growing and going deeper. This is what I call "duality," isn't it? Similarly, China and Japan need deeper cooperation.

Lastly, the development with "duality" is a general and probably mainstream trend. Why? Because people need it. An absolute majority of people need no war. What they need is cooperation in the aforementioned five areas. Thus, Chinese and American political figures are expected to shoulder this responsibility. The cancerous growth of the

US-Japan military alliance should be firmly resisted. Such a clear-minded route is the "new awakening" in the new era. The result will be fundamentally different, whether there is this "new awakening" or not. Effort with the "new awakening" generates wealth, prosperity, development, and naturally a bright future. In contrast, the US-Japan military alliance will only lead to a dead end. The "new awakening" in the complicated situations with "duality" bears the true hope of the Chinese and Japanese peoples.

In summary, my thoughts can be put into six concepts, namely three regions, the New Triangle, two lines, major changes, new awakening, and duality.

And the six concepts are closely related to the ideas I put forth in the early 21st century, including China's peaceful rise, the peaceful rise of a great number of developing countries, and common interests and a community of shared interests around the globe.

I told Yohei Kono that I'm a prudent optimist and confident about a bright future. The "true crucial issues" in the Asia Pacific, including a positive development of the Sino-Japanese relations, would eventually come. Yohei Kono said, "I fully agree with you, Chairman Zheng, that military force will never be the settlement of problems. There's something wrong at present. The role of diplomacy is declining. I think international disputes should be settled by diplomatic means, particularly economic cooperation-based diplomacy."

I held an in-depth talk with Professor Paul Gewirtz from Yale University on March 18, 2015, on the future direction of international relations, particularly of Sino-US relations. We talked about once again the three regions, the New Triangle, and the two lines. I stressed that the root cause of complicated situations on the south line or Asia-Pacific lies in the US. Obama sees the US-Japan military alliance as the "cornerstone" of security in Asia-Pacific, while claiming that Sino-US cooperation lies at the "core" of security in Asia-Pacific. Could the US find uniformity in these two statements?

March 18, 2012. Meeting with Paul Gewirtz, director of the Paul Tsai China Center at Yale Law School, at the CIIDS

Talking about the direction of China, I said that China is sincere, and willing to improve its relationship with the US, to build a new type of major-country relationship. China has never changed and will never change this policy. This is very clear. However, we are facing situations with duality, as mentioned above. So we have to be prepared for two eventualities.

I stressed that Chinese and American leaders need to make a clear analysis of the situations and trends, and make a big decision about the position, significance, and prospects of Sino-US relations. What is this big decision? First of all, it should be clearly defined that Sino-US relations should strategically stand as the "ballast" and "core" of peace and stability in Asia-Pacific. That is, the US-Japan military alliance is not the "cornerstone" of peace and stability in Asia-Pacific. More specifically, it should not authorize Japanese navy and air forces' "patrols" in the South China Sea, in the name of "lifting the ban on collective self-defense from

Japan." Secondly, the signed agreements on Sino-US cooperation shall be substantially carried out. Thirdly, the two countries should reach a serious consensus, based upon the first two points, and taking into consideration situations in the world, particularly in Asia-Pacific. Empty words or idle talk will not help. That is a "big decision" to my understanding.

In fact, when I had a talk with the then US Ambassador to China Max Baucus on February 27, 2015, I talked about this "big decision." I said that as it was called a "big decision," we shouldn't drag on, focus on trivial things, be disingenuous, or play a double-game. Instead, we should base ourselves on reality and see into a long future. We need strategically-important judgment and determination, grasping the overall situation, instead of being bogged down with petty details.

February 27, 2015. Meeting with then US Ambassador to China Max Baucus at the CIIDS

In summary, however complicated the situations are, we need our own judgment. That is, we need to see the duality of international situations, detect new trends in three regions, New Triangle, and two lines, and appropriately deal with inter-state relations, so as to expand common interests and build a community of shared interests.

4. New international relations theory for a new era

This book begins with President Xi Jinping's call for accelerating the construction of socialist philosophy and social science with Chinese characteristics. We are now able to well respond to Xi's call. As "China's path to peaceful rise" is a new century-oriented strategy of China, and "the peaceful rise of all developing countries" a new century-oriented prediction of the world's trends, "a community of shared future" built upon "common interests and a community of shared interests" may be the underlying foundation of a new century-oriented theory of international relations.

There are various theories in the study of international relations, such as realism, liberalism, idealism, and constructivism. Let us just look at the theory of geopolitics that has been in vogue once again in recent years. The theory has had enormous implications on nations' foreign policies. In my analysis of the post-Cold War international situations, I talked about two major points for the international community to maintain international stability, namely power domination, and balance of power, both of which are built upon geopolitics. The balance of power advocated by Nixon and Kissinger focuses on balance and is in essence a geopolitical theory of leading powers contending for domination. This theory has not helped to settle the problems the world faces today. Peace and development remain the main subjects, and peace, development, co-operation and win-win are still the trend. Developing countries are growing powers for world peace and development. "A multipolar pattern of the world" foreseen by Deng Xiaoping is taking shape. In the meantime, the world is never a place of tranquility. Regional hotspot issues are exacerbating. Traditional and non-traditional security issues are intertwined. Many new issues are emerging between developed countries, between developed and developing countries, and between developing countries. We need urgently to decide whether to push the related theory forward in ever-changing international relations.

In fact, as early as in 2002, I already called for expanding "common interests" and building "a community of shared interests" in China's diplomatic practice, as I later wrote in my proposal to the leading department. I drew this idea from my thoughts on Sino-US and Sino-Europe relations and on China's relations with many other developing countries. That is why an ever-stronger China (instead of that underdeveloped country in the early days of its reform and opening up) has been able to follow the path to peaceful rise all through the years. For example, many may find Sino-US relations something quite complicated. But we have seen ever-expanding common interests between the two countries, in such areas as joint effort on dealing with the financial crisis, complementary trade and investment, cooperation in a wide range of areas, and dialogues on hotspot issues. I once said, "When we try harder to expand our common interests, we will see a more solid foundation of common interests and better conditions to build a community of shared interests. There is enormous space and great promising results." It is noteworthy that we actually need to think about how to get along with each other in the 21st century. What is the true meaning of that? I think that means a new century-oriented theory of international relations.

We can say that we will face up to and go beyond geopolitics, by dealing with international relations "to expand common interests and build a community of shared interests." We "face up to" geopolitics, making a clear measure of geopolitical reality, and "go beyond" geopolitics, trying to find common interests and building various communities of shared interests on all levels between different countries, whatever their geographical relationship and political systems are. Therefore, I have offered my opinion to many in regard to expanding common interests and building a community of shared interests.

Another new point to be clarified is that my theory of "common interests and a community of shared interests" is established upon the development of informatization, economic globalization, and multipolarization of the world in the 21st century. Informatization, in particular, is everywhere in our daily life and links interests of different regions, countries, and peoples, via flow of information, goods, and capital. The world is radically changing, isn't it? And this is the new foundation of building "common interests and a community of shared interests" between countries. And economic globalization is irreversible, as economies in the world's market have had something in each other, even though some intend to go back to trade protectionism. An important new trend is emerging, particularly after China put forth its Belt and Road Initiative, and this is the globalization of the marine economy which began on the Atlantic and Pacific 400 years ago and which will develop into a globalization of marine-inland economy never seen in history, as the marine economy is linked up with an inland one. The global market economy is giving rise to "common interests" between different economies and a "community of shared interests" on a large scale never seen before. Many took a dim view of multipolarization a couple of years ago, but now they have to face a new paradigm in which hegemony by a single country is fading away from us. Forming "common interests and a community of shared interests" is the only way for peaceful coexistence of different countries.

President Xi Jinping met in Ufa of Russia with President Islam Karimov of Uzbekistan on 10 July, 2015. Xi stressed that "we need to have a strong awareness of the community with a shared future and common interests and pull together in times of trouble." In his speech at the UK Parliament on October 20, 2015, President Xi stressed that the idea of "the community of common interests" would lead international relations into a new era. He delivered a speech at UN Office at Geneva on January 18, 2017, in which he elaborated on "China's solution" of building a "global community of shared future." In his report at the 19th CPC National Congress, Xi called on "the people of all countries to work together to build a community with a shared future for humanity," and called for "developing global partnerships and expanding the convergence of interests with other countries."[5]

As Chinese, we feel proud that President Xi's idea of "global community of shared future" defines the direction of man's destiny in the 21st century and is highly appreciated by other countries. It has been written into UN documents. The theory of "the common interests and the community of shared interests" established upon the idea of "the community of shared future" has grown from the CPC's consistently-held Marxism adapted to conditions in China, from the CPC's consistently-advocated Five Principles of Peaceful Coexistence and foreign policy of peace, and from the traditional Chinese view of the greater good and shared interests. This theory follows and demonstrates the general trend of international situations in the 21st century. Evidently, it is a new international relations theory for a new era, which illustrates the general trend of the times and represents the interests and will of the overwhelming majority of the people.

---

[5] Xi Jinping: *Secure a Decisive Victory in Building a Moderately Prosperous Society in All Respects and Strive for the Great Success of Socialism with Chinese Characteristics for a New Era – Report to the 19th National Congress of the Communist Party of China*, Foreign Languages Press, 2018, pp. 71-72.

Chapter 6

A New Round of Economic Globalization and New Prospects of China's Peaceful Rise

In the preceding chapter we have, guided by the idea of "global community of shared future," discussed "common interests and a community of shared interests" in the process of economic globalization. Now we would return to China, talking about the trend and prospect of China's peaceful rise. It is interesting to look back into history. China adopted the policy of reform and opening up when the third round of economic globalization began. The country has since been linked with economic globalization. Now, the world is embracing a new round of economic globalization, and socialism with Chinese characteristics is entering into "a new era." The latest round of economic globalization and socialism with Chinese characteristics for a new era complement each other perfectly, meaning China's peaceful rise will inevitably reveal new development prospects both domestically and internationally.

1. Socialism with Chinese characteristics for a new era and the Chinese Dream of national rejuvenation

The 19th CPC National Congress ran from October 18 to 24, 2017, making an incisive summary of the historical changes in the past five years since the 18th CPC National Congress, "With decades of hard work, socialism with Chinese characteristics has crossed the threshold into a new era. This is a new historic juncture in China's development."[1] This is what socialism with Chinese characteristics entering a new era means: The Chinese nation, which since modern times began had endured so much for so long, has achieved a tremendous transformation: It has stood up, grown rich, and is becoming strong; it has come to embrace the brilliant prospects of rejuvenation. Xi Jinping's theory of socialism with Chinese characteristics in the new era is an important part of the theory of socialism with Chinese characteristics and a latest achievement of adapting Marxism to conditions in China.

The Communist Party of China is a political party with strategic thinking. Be it in times of revolution, construction and reform and opening up, or in different stages of the CPC-led undertakings, the Party has always defined its strategic tasks and action plans out of the two overall situations, namely the domestic and international situations. At the very beginning of the reform and opening up of China, Deng Xiaoping put forward a three-step development strategy, with a goal of realizing modernization in China; i.e. to provide the people with ample food and

---

[1] Xi Jinping: *Secure a Decisive Victory in Building a Moderately Prosperous Society in All Respects and Strive for the Great Success of Socialism with Chinese Characteristics for a New Era – Report to the 19th National Congress of the Communist Party of China*, Foreign Languages Press, 2018, p. 13.

clothes by the 1980's, to realize a relatively comfortable life by the 1990's, and based on the first two, to basically realize socialist modernization by the 2050's. With the first two steps in Deng's strategy fulfilled, Jiang Zemin called on "grasping the important strategic opportunities in the first two decades of the 21st century, and building a well-off society in an all-round way," forming the CPC's Two Centenary Goals. At the 18th CPC National Congress, based on the progress in "building a well-off society in an all-round way" since the 16th and 17th National Congresses of the CPC, Hu Jintao put forth the goal of "building an all-around prosperous society." At the 19th CPC National Congress, Xi Jinping stated that China will secure a decisive victory in building a moderately prosperous society in all respects in the coming three years. After this, with another 30 years of work, we will have basically achieved modernization and turned China into a modern socialist country by the mid-21st century.

Based on a comprehensive analysis of the international and domestic environments and the conditions for China's development, we have drawn up a two-stage development plan. In the first stage from 2020 to 2035, we will build on the foundation created by the moderately prosperous society with a further 15 years of hard work to see that socialist modernization is basically realized. That is, the third-step strategic goal of "basically realizing socialist modernization" in Deng Xiaoping's three-step strategy will be fulfilled 15 years ahead of schedule. In the second stage from 2035 to the middle of the 21st century, we will work hard for a further 15 years and develop China into a great modern socialist country that is prosperous, strong, democratic, culturally advanced, harmonious, and beautiful. The Chinese nation will become a proud and active member of the community of nations. This strategic vision illustrates the new task of China's peaceful rise.

To realize our goals of building China into a great modern socialist country, and to fulfill our strategic task of realizing the great rejuvenation of the Chinese nation, the 19th CPC National Congress stresses that as socialism with Chinese characteristics has entered a new era, we must undertake a great struggle with many new contemporary features, launch the great new project of Party building, and advance the great cause of socialism with Chinese characteristics, so as to realize the Chinese Dream of national rejuvenation. As President Xi Jinping has put it, "the Chinese Dream" pursues a stronger and more prosperous country, national rejuvenation, and the people's happiness. Evidently, the Chinese Dream of national rejuvenation is in pursuit of China's peaceful rise against the background of economic globalization. Essentially, we must stand firm in safeguarding China's sovereignty and territorial integrity in the process of economic globalization, and stay on the path of peaceful and civilized development and the socialist modernization of China.

The Chinese people have paid much attention to economic globalization, as they have been longing for modernization. From Lin Zexu of the 1840s to the present generation, five to six generations in China have been in anxious expectation of modernization of the country. Lin is known as a prominent figure of the anti-opium campaigns in his times. But it may be unknown to many that he was also "the first man in modern-day China who opened his eyes to the outside world." Lin had English newspapers read to him and then briefed to the emperor. Lin was the first man in China who seriously thought about learning from the industrial revolution in the West. The goal of modernization was not fulfilled by the five to six generations over a period of more than 150 years. But with 40 years of reform and opening up, we can now proudly say that we are reaching the goal of modernization in China, and realizing the Chinese Dream of national rejuvenation.

All who are free from prejudice and respect history and facts can see that the Chinese Dream is the logical outcome of and requisite for China's path. In the meantime, we must unremittingly adhere to and remain committed to the path of socialism with Chinese characteristics. The practice of reform and opening up has shown that this path has made China act as never before, develop rapidly, and grow prosperous and strong with each passing day. Also, China has seen enormous advantage and gained strong vitality from reform and opening up, in contrast to various "-isms" that are plagued with changing regimes or mired in crises "when all else fails." History has shown that the path of socialism with Chinese characteristics is the only path to the glorious future of the rejuvenation of the Chinese nation.

That is to say, self-development is the key to realize the Chinese Dream. It is more clearly seen when the Chinese Dream is put against the broad background of economic globalization: In energy consumption, we cannot afford an American Dream of an average annual consumption of 25 barrels of oil in the process of modernization for a long time. In population movement, we will not have a European dream to realize self-development by setting up overseas colonies around the globe as the Europeans did in modern history. In enhancing the overall national strength, we absolutely will not have a USSR dream of stubborn arms race or "exporting revolution" to others. It is important that we proceed from China's national conditions in the primary stage of socialism, keep clear-minded in front of challenges, and strive to realize "three step-overs": We need to step over the old track the Western powers took in the modern era to complete the process of industrialization through colonial pillage of resources around the world; to step over the old track militarist Germany and Japan took to re-divide up the world by launching a war; and to step over the old track hegemonies took to contend for dominance and sphere of influence. Standing firm on the path of peaceful rise is the only way to realize the "three step-overs" or the Chinese Dream, in contrast to the modernization of Europe and the US.

2. Xi Jinping's two speeches in answer to "where will economic globalization go?"

The Communist Party of China faces a great challenge in the new era: "Where will economic globalization go?" As President Xi Jinping stressed in his keynote speech at the opening session of the World Economic Forum Annual Meeting on January 17, 2017, "World history shows that the road of human civilization has never been a smooth one, and that mankind has made progress by surmounting difficulties. No difficulty, however daunting, will stop mankind from advancing. When encountering difficulties, we should not complain about ourselves, blame others, lose confidence or run away from responsibilities. We should join hands and rise to the challenge. History is created by the brave. Let us boost confidence, take actions and march arm-in-arm toward a bright future."[2]

At the key moment when the international community was debating the future of economic globalization, Chinese President Xi Jinping visited Davos, a beautiful town in the Alps and delivered a keynote speech at the opening session of the World Economic Forum Annual Meeting on January 17, 2017, elaborating on China's view on this round of economic globalization. He delivered a keynote speech at the UN Office at Geneva the next day. Xi's two keynote speeches addressed the globally-concerned issue of "uncertainties of the world" and answered the fundamental question "Where will economic globalization and the world go?" Xi's speeches caught the attention of the entire world.

This round of economic globalization started in the 1970s. Roughly speaking, the four-decade economic globalization which has experienced many ups and downs has boosted great economic development and

---

[2] *People's Daily*, January 18, 2017.

given rise to numerous problems. This is the "duality" of economic globalization. This round of US-led economic globalization has contributed enormously to the world's economic development. Nonetheless, it was born with evident defects: Virtualization of the economy has built a wide channel for speculation; employment has become more difficult in industrial hollowing-out; and exacerbating social polarization has intensified populism and nationalism. Such problems are surfacing and breaking out in some developed countries now, leaving impacts on the entire world.

We may deal with the situation in two ways. One is to find a way out through trade protectionism, in the name of "preference" for one's own country. The other is, to the call for "a global community of shared future," to push economic globalization into a new stage, through a rational layout of social productivity, including stocks and innovation, a reasonable integration of financial capital and real economy, and optimization of global governance and systematic reform of economic and political orders. The former is a route of retrogression, by which we cannot solve problems met in the process of economic globalization. It is obviously not the correct way out. The latter faces up to and tries to find adequate solutions for new problems emerging in the process of economic globalization. This is the correct choice. "China's proposition" put forward in Chinese President Xi's speech is a good representative of this approach.

President Xi said, in his keynote speeches at Davos and Geneva, "Where will economic globalization and the world go?" – the world's biggest concern at present – and put forth "China's proposition" that has been established on an incisive analysis of historic experience and practical problems.

First of all, President Xi talked about the general trend of the world today from the angle of history. As he said, to answer the question, "we need to get clear about a fundamental issue: Where did we come from? Where are we now? And where are we going?" He continued, "Over the past century and more, mankind has gone through bloody hot wars and the chilling Cold War, but also achieved remarkable development and huge progress. In the first half of last century, mankind suffered the scourges of two world wars, and the people yearned for the end of war and the advent of peace. In the 1950s and 1960s, people in colonies awakened and fought to shake off shackles and achieve independence. Since the end of the Cold War, people have pursued a shared aspiration, namely, to expand cooperation and promote common development." We can gain a clear understanding, with such a comparison in a larger historical context, of problems in the world and economic globalization today. As President Xi said, "Mankind is in an era of major development as well as profound transformation and change. The trend toward multi-polarity and economic globalization is surging. IT application in social development and cultural diversity are making continued progress. A new round of scientific and industrial revolution is in the making. Interconnection and interdependence between countries are crucial for human survival. The forces for peace far outweigh factors causing war, and the trend of our times toward peace, development, cooperation and win-win outcomes has gained stronger momentum."[3]

Then, President Xi made a scientific and specific analysis of problems emerging in economic globalization. He pointed out, "Today, we also live in a world of contradictions. And (various factors) have all added to the uncertainties of the world." Xi made it clear that "To answer this question, one must first track the source of the problem." In response to those who blame economic globalization for the chaos in the world, he said, "many of the problems troubling the world are not caused by economic globalization. For instance, the refugee waves from the Middle East and North Africa in recent years have become a global

[3] *People's Daily*, January 20, 2017.

concern. Several million people have been displaced, and some small children lost their lives while crossing the rough sea. This is indeed heartbreaking. It is war, conflict and regional turbulence that have created this problem, and its solution lies in making peace, promoting reconciliation and restoring stability. The international financial crisis is another example. It is not an inevitable outcome of economic globalization; rather, it is the consequence of excessive chase of profit by financial capital and grave failure of financial regulation. Just blaming economic globalization for the world's problems is inconsistent with reality, and it will not help solve the problems." Xi put it in a vivid way, "Whether you like it or not, the global economy is the big ocean that you cannot escape from. Any attempt to cut off the flow of capital, technologies, products, industries and people between economies, and channel the waters in the ocean back into isolated lakes and creeks is simply not possible. Indeed, it runs counter to the historical trend."[4]

In the meantime, President Xi stressed that economic globalization is a double-edged sword, and we should make a dialectic analysis of its "duality." On the one hand, as Xi put it, economic globalization, as a result of growing social productivity, is a natural outcome of scientific and technological progress, not something created by any individuals or any countries. Economic globalization has propelled global growth and facilitated the movement of goods and capital, advances in science, technology and civilization, and interactions among peoples. He said, "Economic globalization, a surging historical trend, has greatly facilitated trade, investment, flow of people and technological advances. Since the turn of the century, under the auspices of the UN and riding on the waves of economic globalization, the international community has set the Millennium Development Goals and the 2030 Agenda for Sustainable Develop-

[4] *People's Daily*, January 18, 2017.

ment. Thanks to these initiatives, 1.1 billion people have been lifted out of poverty, 1.9 billion people now have access to safe drinking water, 3.5 billion people have gained access to the Internet, and the goal has been set to eradicate extreme poverty by 2030."[5] On the other hand, as Xi pointed, it is true that economic globalization has created new problems. He particularly stressed, "The global economy has remained sluggish for quite some time. The gap between the poor and the rich and between the South and the North is widening. The root cause is that the three critical issues in the economic sphere have not been effectively addressed." "First, lack of robust driving forces for global growth makes it difficult to sustain the steady growth of the global economy." "Second, inadequate global economic governance makes it difficult to adapt to new developments in the global economy." "Third, uneven global development makes it difficult to meet people's expectations for better lives."[6]

Then, President Xi stressed that we should be brave to face up to problems, solve problems, and jointly meet challenges, so as to promote economic globalization. He made it clear, "At present, the most pressing task before us is to steer the global economy out of difficulty." "The history of mankind tells us that problems are not to be feared. What should concern us is refusing to face up to problems and not knowing what to do about them. In the face of both opportunities and challenges of economic globalization, the right thing to do is to seize every opportunity, jointly meet challenges and chart the right course for economic globalization."[7] He also warned, "Voices against globalization have laid bare pitfalls in the process of economic globalization that we need to take seriously."[8]

---

[5] *People's Daily*, January 20, 2017.

[6] *People's Daily*, January 18, 2017.

[7] *Ibid.*

[8] *Ibid.*

What was the proposition President Xi presented in his speeches at the World Economic Forum and UN Office at Geneva?

"Pass on the torch of peace from generation to generation, sustain development and make civilization flourish: This is what people of all countries long for; it is also the responsibility statesmen of our generation ought to shoulder. And China's proposition is: build a community with a shared future for mankind and achieve shared and win-win development."[9] "A global community of shared future" in "China's proposition" is the core idea and statement of President Xi's speeches. As Xi put it in his speech, diversity of human civilizations not only defines our world, but also drives progress of mankind. There are more than 200 countries and regions, over 2,500 ethnic groups and multiple religions in our world. Different histories, national conditions, ethnic groups and customs give birth to different civilizations, making the world a colorful one. There is no such thing as a superior or inferior civilization, and civilizations are different only in identity and location. Diversity of civilizations should not be a source of global conflict; rather, it should be an engine driving the advance of human civilizations. Then he continued to say that building a community of shared future is an exciting goal, and it requires efforts from generation to generation. China is ready to work with all other UN member states as well as international organizations and agencies to advance the great cause of building a global community of shared future.

The practice in the past 40 years or so shows that all countries, whatever their histories, cultures, social systems or ideologies, can always identify common interests in the process of economic globalization, and on this basis build a community of shared interests, which can lay a solid foundation of interests for a global community of shared future. Presi-

---

[9] *People's Daily*, January 20, 2017.

dent Xi has many times linked "a community of shared interests" with "a community with a shared future," charting the right course for the world. His "global community of shared future" shines over the correct way ahead for world peace, development and economic globalization, and makes clear that the new round of economic globalization should not follow the criterion of a single country; instead, it should follow shared interests and future. Just as President Xi pointed, "We should strengthen coordination and improve governance so as to ensure sound growth of economic globalization and make it open, inclusive, balanced and beneficial to all. We should both make the cake bigger and share it fairly to ensure justice and equity."

In short, "to build a global community of shared future and achieve win-win and shared development" is the most remarkable feature of boosting the new round of economic globalization in a multi-polar world, and should be the goal of forming "the common interests" and "a community of shared interests" in this new round of economic globalization.

3. The Belt and Road Initiative and a new round of economic globalization

While countries were in a heated discussion about "where economic globalization is going" and "where the world is going," the Belt and Road Forum for International Cooperation was convened in Beijing from May 14 to 15, 2017. People noticed that over 1,500 distinguished guests from more than 130 countries gathered for this unprecedented event, including heads of state and government from 29 countries and leaders and representatives of over 70 major international organizations such as the

United Nations. The Forum took place at a time when anti-globalization trends surged under the banners of trade protectionism and populism and when all countries cared about the direction of economic globalization. Therefore, people all expected it to inject new momentum to a new round of economic globalization.

The "Belt and Road" is the abbreviation for the Silk Road Economic Belt and the 21st Century Maritime Silk Road, initiatives proposed by President Xi Jinping respectively in Kazakhstan and then in Indonesia in September and October 2013. The proposal of the Belt and Road Initiative highlights the call for a key turning point after the third round of economic globalization had developed for nearly 40 years. This is, I believe, the right historical starting point for the birth of the grand vision of the Belt and Road Initiative.

September 19, 2017. Addressing the audience at the Media Cooperation Forum on Belt and Road in Dunhuang, Gansu Province

It has been only four years since the Belt and Road Initiative was proposed, but it has received a positive response and participation from over 100 countries and international organizations. Why has it caused such a sensation? An overview of today's economic changes in the world will offer a better understanding. The third round of economic globalization on the one hand, has seen escalating conflicts between developed economies, and on the other, peaceful rising of developing economies. As the latest predictions of the International Monetary Fund indicate, the global economy is expected to achieve an average annual growth rate of nearly 3.6%, slightly better than 3.2% in the past two years. This is obviously good news. If we further analyse the structure of the data, it can then be found that developing economies are growing faster than developed economies. The rate is likely to reach 4.6%, more than twice as much as the 2% growth rate of developed economies. A historical comparison of economic aggregates between the two blocs is even more thought-provoking. In Purchasing Power Parity terms, the ratio of the economic aggregate of developed economies to that of developing ones was 64:36 in 1980; and 50:50 in 2007. As estimated, it will be reversed to 41:59 in 2018.

And this means that the shift in the focus of the world economy that began in the first decade in the 21st century is likely to gain further momentum, including great development of developing economies and redevelopment of developed economies, in the process of major long-cycle changes in the world economy in the 2nd to the 4th decades of the 21st century. This will usher in a new round of economic globalization. I believe that this is also a historic condition conducive to the birth of the grand plan of the Belt and Road.

From its proposal to development, what are the fundamental historical features of the grand plan of the Belt and Road Initiative? Can we say that the collaborative effort across Eurasia shows that economic globalization is making great strides from marine economic globalization toward unprecedented economic connectivity both on the sea and on the land? The past rounds of economic globalization, from the Atlantic to the Pacific, were generally globalization of the marine economy. Today, things are completely different. In the Belt and Road Initiative, the inland economy will become a second major force of economic globalization. The Belt and Road Initiative integrates new and old tools such as container sea transportation, expressways, high-speed rail, air transportation, the Internet and modern online financial products, builds great passages of logistics, capital, science and technology and culture, and connects marine and inland economies comprehensively, thereby driving the economic upgrade of eastern, central and western China as well as economic cooperation and development across Eurasia from and to the African and American continents. Herein lie the new features of the new round of economic globalization.

We remember, when the Belt and Road Initiative was first proposed, some said that for China it was a means of overcapacity relocation; some called it the Chinese Marshall Plan; some even accused it of neo-colonialism, or regarded it as China's attempt to repel Europe and the United States. All these theories are based on the narrow philosophy of zero-sum game and manifest the ignorance that the grand plan of the Belt and Road Initiative is essentially about cooperation, about common interests, and about a community of shared interests and shared future. It is a strategic vision of "collaborative construction" proposed in line with the historic trend of the new round of economic globalization.

Of course we should be aware that the Belt and Road Initiative which calls for joint effort by many countries is by no means an easy task and cannot be accomplished at a single stroke. We should be mentally prepared for sustained effort, which determines that we must collaborate, with every party dedicated to the Belt and Road Initiative. Moreover, the collaborative relationship must be long-term.

At the Belt and Road Forum for International Cooperation on May

14, 2017, President Xi Jinping expounded in his keynote speech the vision of achieving shared growth through discussion and collaboration in the framework of the Belt and Road Initiative. He said that we should build the Belt and Road into a road for peace, a road of prosperity, a road of opening up, a road of innovation and a road connecting civilizations.

To build a road for peace means that we should construct a new type of international relations with cooperation and sharing at the core and build partnerships characterized by dialogue without confrontation, partnership without alliance. All countries should respect each other's sovereignty, dignity and territorial integrity, respect each other's development path and social system and respect each other's core interests and major concerns; foster the vision of common, comprehensive, cooperative and sustainable security, and create a security environment built and shared by all. We should work to resolve hotspot issues through political means, and promote mediation in the spirit of justice. We should intensify counter-terrorism efforts, address both its symptoms and root causes, and strive to eradicate poverty, backwardness and social injustice.

To build a road of prosperity means that we should focus on the fundamental issue of development, release the growth potential of various countries, and achieve economic integration and interconnected development and deliver benefits to all. All countries achieve connectivity and maintain the dynamic for economic growth by means of industrial cooperation, financial guarantee, infrastructure connectivity, etc.

To build a road of opening up means that the Belt and Road Initiative should be an open one which will achieve both economic growth and balanced development. All countries should build an open platform of cooperation and uphold an open world economy; jointly create an environment that will facilitate opening up and development; establish a fair, equitable and transparent system of international trade and investment

January 17, 2013. On a field trip to Yunnan Province

rules; and boost the orderly flow of production factors, efficient resources allocation and full market integration. All countries should grow open economies based on their national conditions, participate in global governance and provide public goods, and build a broad community of shared interests. While promoting liberalization and facilitation of trade and investment, we should also focus on resolving issues such as imbalances in development, difficulties in governance, digital divide, and income disparity, and make economic globalization open, inclusive, balanced and beneficial to all.

To build a road of innovation means that we should sustain growth through innovation. We should pursue innovation-driven development and intensify cooperation in frontier areas such as the digital economy, artificial intelligence, nanotechnology, and quantum computing, and advance the development of big data, cloud computing, and smart cities so as to turn them into a digital "silk road" of the 21st century. We should spur the full integration of science and technology with industries and finance, improve the environment for innovation, and pool resources for innovation. We should create space and build workshops for young people of various countries to cultivate entrepreneurship in this age of the Internet and help realize their dreams. Meanwhile, we should pursue the new vision of green development and a way of life and work that is green, low-carbon, circular and sustainable. Efforts should be made to strengthen cooperation in ecological and environmental protection and build a sound ecosystem so as to realize the 2030 Sustainable Development Goals.

To build a road connecting civilizations means that in pursuing the Belt and Road Initiative, we should ensure that when it comes to different civilizations, exchange will replace estrangement, mutual learning will replace clashes, and coexistence will replace the sense of superiority. This will boost mutual understanding, mutual respect and mutual trust among different countries. We should establish a multi-tiered mechanism for cultural and people-to-people exchanges, build more cooperation platforms, and open more cooperation channels. Educational cooperation should be promoted. Think tanks should play a better role. In the cultural, sports and health sectors, new cooperation models should be created to facilitate projects with concrete benefits. Historical and cultural heritage should be fully tapped to jointly develop tourist products and protect heritage in ways that preserve the distinctive features of the Silk Road.

We should, through such international cooperation, build the Belt and Road into a road for peace, a road of prosperity, a road of opening up, a road of innovation, and a road connecting civilizations, and make it a strong driving force and an important sign for the advent of a new round of economic globalization. It can be said this is where lies the significance of the historic meeting in Beijing of the heads of state and government and leaders of the international organizations.

4. To build a people-centered cyberpower and the new round of economic globalization

China's modernization associated with the new round of economic globalization must take into consideration the new situation of incessant changes in information and Internet technology in the present-day world. This requires that industrialization and informatization be developed simultaneously and combined closely – the unprecedented historic feat in world history China must accomplish in the first half of the 21st century as a late-coming power in modernization.

The rapid development of the Internet in China is a big event. Not only is it a profound revolution in science and technology, but it manifests a new awakening of human civilization and heralds a brand-new epoch for human civilization. President Xi Jinping points out with broad world vision and keen political savvy that "from the perspective of the history of social development, humanity, which has been through the agricultural revolution and the industrial revolution, is now experiencing the Information Revolution." More than 20 years after China had Internet access, 700 million netizens enjoy a new life transformed by the new space and platforms of the Internet; moreover, the whole society has felt the tremendous changes in interactivity, lifestyle and means of production, as well as the subsequent great strides in economy, politics, military, culture and other sectors. Such major historic changes vividly reflect that the Chinese, who missed the opportunities of the industrial revolution in modern history, have seized the historical opportunities of the Information Revolution today.

November 17, 2016. Speaking at the International High-Level Think Tank Forum on the Internet, part of the Third World Internet Conference

In recent years, President Xi Jinping has delivered a series of important speeches on IT application, cyberization and the development of the Internet and IT, which have set forth with deep insight the concept of people-centered orientation of the Internet and IT. Revolving on the concept, he systematically expounds on a series of major issues such as building a good ecosystem for the Internet, making breakthroughs in core technologies, properly handling the relationship between security and development, strengthening the sense of mission and responsibility of Internet companies, and providing talent support for Internet development. In view of the rapid development of the Internet worldwide, given the new circumstances and issues confronting China's cybersecurity and IT application, it has become more evident that to build a people-centered cyberpower meets the demand of the new round of globalization and a crucial strategic component of China's "peaceful rise" initiative.

We are in a changeable new era transformed by the on-going Information Revolution. The correct perception of, and strategies for, the era is the prerequisite for the healthy development of China's Internet and IT. At the Symposium on Cybersecurity and IT Application, President Xi Jinping articulately and firmly stressed, "If China's Internet and IT undertakings are to develop, it is essential that they revolve around the people." Our Internet and IT undertakings are essentially of the people and they are boosted for the people.

First, China's Internet undertakings are of the people. The assertion that they should revolve around the people dictates that they are "for the people in nature" rather than otherwise. In today's world, it is a cardinal question of right or wrong whether the era of the Internet and IT application is an era of power hegemony or a people-centered one. Since the birth of the Internet, countries have divergent basic standpoints and guidelines on this issue. Some use the Internet to control world opinion; a few have even used it as a tool to interfere with other countries' domestic affairs or even to subvert other countries' governments. Such practices have deviated from the zeitgeist represented by the Internet. We must consciously build a people-centered Internet, with the firm belief that Internet undertakings are great undertakings of the people and the era of the Internet is a great time of the people. Such is the outlook of the Chinese on Internet development.

Secondly, China develops Internet undertakings so that the Internet can better benefit the people. One fundamental guideline runs through President Xi Jinping's important speeches, that is, "build the Internet well for the people." The development of China's Internet is intended, at a policy level, for China to seize the opportunities, catch up with the times and achieve the rejuvenation of the Chinese nation; and at a practical level, to provide the people with useful, affordable quality information services, "thus enabling millions upon millions of Chinese people to gain a stronger sense of benefit from the development of the Internet." What is particularly worth mentioning is that President Xi has profound affection for the broad masses of people in rural areas. He points out specifically that "the development of Internet infrastructure in the countryside is an area in which we are falling short." He requires that we should "accelerate the development of the Internet in the countryside and extend the effective coverage of fiber-optic networks and broadband in rural areas." This demonstrates China's determination to resolve the digital divide that has been haunting the world by resolving the issue of urban Internet access. Consideration has always been given to "benefiting the people" from the guideline to specific requirements. These are the values we Chinese have regarding Internet development.

Thirdly, the purpose of building a good ecosystem of the Internet is to give better play to the role of the Internet in guiding and reflecting public opinion. The Internet is a large platform of social information. From there millions upon millions of netizens acquire and exchange information. This will exert significant influence upon their means of knowledge acquisition, thinking and values, especially their views on the state, society, work and life. As President Xi Jinping says, the majority of netizens are common people from different places with different experiences, so it is certain that their opinions and views vary and there are also complaints and biases. How can we deal with the situation? Some hold that the Internet is complicated and hard to manage and it would be better to ban and close it for good. Responding to this opinion President Xi states definitely, "This sort of argument is incorrect, and is also not a way to resolve problems. China's great open gate cannot be closed and will not be closed." He further points out that "cyberspace is a common virtual home for millions upon millions of people" and "netizens are members of the general public. If members of the public go online, so does public opinion." Therefore, he requires that Party and government authorities and their leaders should use the Internet to understand public opinion and stay in touch with the people online. In particular, he also stresses that they should have "more tolerance and patience" for netizens' opinions and views. "To attain our goals, we will need to form concentric circles both online and offline." This is the outlook of the Chinese on people going online.

Lastly, it is the people that propel the progress of Internet and IT undertakings. The people-centered guideline of Internet is upheld not only for the people but also by the people. Both Internet development and cyberspace governance depend upon the people. Efforts should be made to boost the shift of Internet undertakings in governance from unidirectional administration to bidirectional interaction. President Xi Jinping further stresses that, first, the people's initiative should be mobilized and the sense of mission and responsibility of Internet enterprises strengthened; and, secondly, the people's supervision of the Internet should be accepted. "Not only must we welcome well-meant criticism and public oversight online, but we must study it and take it into account, regardless of whether it is directed at the work of the Party and government or at officials personally, and regardless of whether it is mild-mannered or unpleasant to hear." We are glad to see that China has issued a series of important decisions and laws concerning the development of Internet, including *Outline of the National Strategy of Innovation-Driven Development, Outline of the National Informatization Development Strategy, National Cyberspace Security Strategy, Strategy for Cyberspace International Collaboration, Cybersecurity Law of the People's Republic of China,* and *Big Data Development Plan (2016-2020)*.

Today, the Chinese people are embracing the new era of the Internet and IT application with confidence. In the face of challenges of the Information Revolution, only by embracing the era can we develop China. As President Xi Jinping states, "Our country's economic development has entered a new normal, the new normal requires new drivers, and the Internet can have great potential in this area."

Then, how can we rely on the Internet to form new drivers in the context of the economic new normal? President Xi Jinping's view that we should "open up the information 'artery' of economic and social development" is inspiring and enlightening. This means "making rigorous efforts to integrate the Internet more deeply into the real economy, using information flows to facilitate the flow of technology, capital, talent, and materials, and improve resource allocation and increase total factor productivity, so as to develop innovatively, transform the economic growth model, and restructure the economy." Just as the theory of opening up the conception (*ren*) and governor (*du*) vessels[10] in Chinese medicine, opening up the great information artery is becoming a new driver of Chinese economic development in the new normal.

First of all, this new driver manifests itself in boosting the contemporary Chinese people's productivity. The Information Revolution ensuing the industrial revolution is causing great changes to productivity and production modes. The new type of productivity driven by Internet and big data technologies will create infinite new resources, new wealth and new space for humanity. Data can be used repeatedly and information shared – this is the essential characteristic with which cyberspace exceeds physical space. It can also be a powerful lever that moves the human race toward a new civilization.

Secondly, the new driver is reflected by the contemporary Chinese people's national defence capabilities. Information technology has given birth to information weaponry, forming information advantages and even altering the patterns of war and defence. Meanwhile, after the Inter-

[10] According to Chinese medicine, the conception and governor vessels, located at different acupuncture points, regulate respectively the flow of *yin* and *yang* energy in the human body. If they are opened up and connected, all vessels are connected.

net space become the fifth-dimension territory, cyberspace security has emerged as the tier-one security threat to sovereign states. Well known global security incidents have once and again proven that states have borders but cyber threats do not. In the cyber world, no one can be safe alone. Developing a cyberspace defence force and building a new defence system is one of China's responsibilities as a power in carrying out international cooperation and maintaining peace and development in the world cyberspace.

Thirdly, the new driver is shown in contemporary Chinese people's cultural strengths. Cyberization enlightens people and improves their qualities and abilities. The amount of information modern people are exposed to far exceeds that in any previous time. Television, telephone and data have merged into one big network; the "cyber genre," encompassing new media, we media, and ideographic Internet language and memes, has taken full advantage of their fragmental form to spread, far exceeding traditional media in popularity and influence. Its influence upon netizens, especially the younger generation, can be compared to that of the vernacular movement one century ago. Furthermore, today's "cyber genre" is worldwide, thus providing an important opportunity for the convergence of the rejuvenation of the Chinese civilization and world trends. Internet culture and creative and cultural industries have emerged, and the Internet has acquired an inestimable capacity of transcultural transmission.

Lastly, the driver also manifests itself in contemporary Chinese people's governance capacity. Today, a large proportion of the Chinese people are moving in many ways and in large numbers, across regions, between rural and urban areas, among industries, and between home and abroad, amidst great social changes. The "human flow" has been brought about by the major changes to economic components, ways of employment, forms of organization, etc. in the vast space of great social changes and massive population migration created by opening up and the socialist market economy. The "human flow" with historic characteristics of reform and opening up is unprecedented and peerless in scale in Chinese and world history. The massive "human flow," coupled with active "capital flow," "material flow," "information flow" and "intellectual flow," has made up a great trend whose influence reaches every aspect of contemporary Chinese society. In the new era, in the historical process of industrialization, urbanization, marketization, informatization and internationalization when brand-new social changes reach new levels, on the solid material foundation of adherence to developing social productivity, after nearly three decades of "organization" following the founding of PRC (the first phase) and over three decades of "energization" since the beginning of reform and opening up (the second phase), contemporary China is expected to enter a brand-new stage that is more active, more orderly and more harmonious. In the new era, the Chinese have conducted themselves properly, further cultivated "inner strength" and truly give a good play to their governance capacity, promoting the modernization of the state governance system and governance capacity, and improving and developing the socialist system with Chinese characteristics. Then China, the power that rises peacefully in the first half of the 21st century, will become "an amiable power" as Chairman Mao described in the 1950s.[11]

Here one thing that particularly needs emphasis is that the development of the Internet and IT industries has revealed that productivity is always the fundamental driving force of social development and progress, and new productivity is always the fundamental new driving force of social development and progress. Social development and progress

---

[11] Mao Zedong: "Outline for the Speech at the Meeting of Nanjing and Shanghai Party Officials," *Manuscripts of Mao Zedong Since 1949*, Vol. VI, Central Party Literature Press, 1992, Chinese edition, p. 405.

cannot be achieved without the development and progress of productivity. The law for the development of the Internet and IT industries also tells us that creativity is the only criterion for the development and progress of productivity. Lack of innovation means stagnation, which leads to elimination. Quite a few renowned enterprises and entrepreneurs in and out of China have constantly been marginalized by the chasing pack because of their failure to see the special quality of the Internet. Though in the area of the Internet and IT application China is considerably behind developed countries, China does not lack creative genes. The Chinese nation is a highly creative people. In recent years, many innovations in the sector of the Internet and IT application are already leading the world, including innovation of online business models, products, marketing, management, and finance. All enterprises good at advancing the "Internet Plus" and "Plus the Internet" are likely to open up the space and potential of sustainable development brought about by shared economy. If we can grasp the general trend and direction with a clear mind, new opportunities are ahead.

In the "first half" of the Internet since China's full access to the Internet in 1994, the Communist Party of China has keenly seized the rare opportunities which history has given China and is now leading the Chinese people in the first phalanx of the world sunrise industry – a position rare in modern Chinese history. In the "second half" of China's development in the Internet and IT application, we are confident that under the leadership of the CPC Central Committee with Xi Jinping at the core, the Chinese people will certainly make more splendid achievements.

In brief, we are facing a brand-new era in the on-going Information Revolution. The new era calls for a new awakening and new space to unfold new civilisation. In the making of the new civilization, the productivity, defence capabilities, cultural strengths and governance capacity will be connected and integrated with the Internet, penetrating and transforming each other. It is certain that unprecedented human wonders will be created.

October 29, 2012. On a field trip to the Irkeshtam Pass, Xinjiang

5. The themes of the time remaining peace and development and the pursuit of the road of peaceful rise

Today, to uphold peace and development – the themes of the time, China must face various new circumstances, new situations and new issues confronting peace and development worldwide and stick to and forge ahead along the development road of peaceful rise.

As said above, what is crucial to China's development is that the Chinese people blazed a development path under the leadership of the Communist Party of China, suited to China's national conditions. The development path of peaceful rise is a brand-new path for independently building socialism with Chinese characteristics in the process of linking to rather than detaching itself from economic globalization. China will continue along this path for more than 30 years until the mid-21st century when China achieves full modernization and can be said to rise in the truest sense. Compared with economic globalization in the past nearly four decades, the new round of economic globalization will certainly adhere to the principles of trade and investment liberalization and facilitation. Meanwhile, it will shed the fetters of the old stereotypes which split and pit against each other's domestic and global interests, domestic capital gains and people's benefits; resolve the issues of imbalanced development, governance dilemma, digital divide, distribution gap, and make economic globalization open, inclusive, balanced and beneficial to all. China's path of peaceful rise connected with rather than detached from such economic globalization is certain to unfold new prospects guided by the concept of the global community of shared future.

First, the new prospect of China's peaceful rise is new in that China aims to build this community by sticking to the new path of peaceful rise in the context of world polarization, economic globalization, social informatization and cultural diversification, with peace and development as the theme of the time.

The Chinese have always believed that China will do well only when the world does well, and vice versa. President Xi says in his speech at the United Nations Office at Geneva that China will never change its commitment to upholding world peace, to pursuing common development, to fostering partnerships and to multilateralism. This shows to the world that China will unswervingly follow the path of peaceful development. In fact, over the past millennia, peace has been in the veins of the Chinese nation and in the genes of the Chinese people. Hundreds of years ago, when China was so prosperous that its GDP accounted for 30% of the world total, it never invaded other countries or expanded its territory. In the 100 years following the 1840 Opium War, China was invaded, oppressed and ravaged, suffering from warfare and chaos. Confucius says, "What you do not want done to yourself, do not do to others." The Chinese people are convinced that only peace can bring about prosperous development. Since the founding of the People's Republic of China in 1949, particularly after the beginning of reform and opening up, China has always stuck to the independent foreign policy of peace and sought friendly cooperation with all countries on the basis of the Five Principles of Peaceful Coexistence. China has been the first to make building partnership a guiding principle for relations between different countries. So far, it has built partnerships of different forms with more than 90 countries and regional organizations. China will further expand its ties, linking it with friends across the world in the process of peaceful rise. China will unswervingly follow the path of peaceful development. To whatever level China develops, China will never seek hegemony, or expansion, or sphere of influence. History has proven and will continue to prove this.

Moreover, as we are aware, the world is undergoing drastic historic changes. From the Cold War between the two poles in the East and West, to the pattern of "one superpower among several great powers" after the end of the two-pole pattern, to G20 collegiality and to the formation of a multi-polar world pattern, the international community is progressing step by step according to such historical logic. With the advance of the Belt and Road Initiative, the economic globalization dominated by Western developed countries represented by the United States is evolving into economic globalization characterized by achieving shared growth through consultation and collaboration. What is particularly worth mentioning is that in the historic transition China upholds the principle of the "global community of shared future" and will forge ahead along the road of peaceful rise. As President Xi Jinping points out in his speech at the United Nations Office in Geneva, China "will continue to pursue a win-win strategy of opening up, share our development opportunities with other countries and welcome them aboard the fast train of China's development." "Between 1950 and 2016, China provided foreign countries with over RMB 400 billion of aid, and we will continue to increase assistance to others as our ability permits. Since the outbreak of the international financial crisis, China has contributed to over 30% of global growth each year on average. In the coming five years, China will import US$8 trillion worth of goods, attract US$600 billion foreign investment, make US$750 billion outbound investment, and Chinese tourists will make 700 million outbound visits. All this will bring more development opportunities to other countries."[12] The Chinese government has officially declared that it will strive to set up a framework for major-country relations featuring overall stability and balanced development and build relationships with developing and neighboring countries, which include: 1) China will actively build a new model of relationship with the United States; 2) China will develop a comprehensive strategic partnership of cooperation with Russia; 3) China will construct partnerships for peace, growth, reform and civilization with Europe; 4) China will establish partnerships of solidarity and cooperation with the other BRICS countries; 5) China will continue to uphold justice and friendship and pursue shared interests, and boost pragmatic cooperation with other developing countries to achieve common development; 6) China will further enhance mutually beneficial cooperation with our neighbors under the principle of amity, sincerity, mutual benefit and inclusiveness; 7) China will pursue common development with African countries in a spirit of sincerity, focus on results, affinity and good faith; 8) China will elevate our comprehensive cooperative partnership with Latin America to a higher level; and 9) as a founding member of the United Nations and the first coun-

[12] *People's Daily*, January 20, 2017.

try to put its signature on the UN Charter, China will firmly uphold the international system with the UN at its core, the basic norms governing international relations embodied in the purposes and principles of the UN Charter, the authority and stature of the UN, and its core role in international affairs.

To sum up, as President Xi Jinping expounds at the CPC in Dialogue with World Political Parties High-Level Meeting, building a global community of shared future is in essence to connect the prospects and future of every nation and country closely together, share weal and woe, turn planet earth into a harmonious family and make the beautiful life desired by the peoples in the world a reality. Our goal is to build a world free of fear and safe for everyone, a world of common prosperity with no poverty, an open, inclusive world, and a clean and beautiful world with picturesque scenery. He stresses, as long as all parties uphold the concept of the global community of shared future, plan and practice together, persist in efforts bit by bit, and make unremitting efforts day by day, the goal will certainly be achieved. These important thoughts unveil the new prospects of China's peaceful rise path in the tide of the new round of economic globalization.

Secondly, the new prospect of China's peaceful rise is new in that China will promote innovation-driven, coordinated, green, open and shared development with the people at the center and continue its effort to blaze a new path of peaceful rise.

In the process of China's peaceful rise, we have over the years encountered challenges in resources – particularly energy, challenges in development environment – particularly eco-environment, and challenges of inadequately balanced economic and social development. China ranks very low in the world in terms of per capita share of resources. However, due to its rapid growth and generally low technological level, Chinese manufacturing is in the front rank in terms of unit and total resource consumption – energy consumption included. To make things worse, the migration of world manufacturing to China in great quantities has also brought a certain degree of "energy consumption transfer." As a result, the shortage of resources, especially energy sources, has become an issue disrupting China's peaceful rise. The problems which appear in the course of China's rapid industrialization and modernization, such as severe environmental pollution, ecological deterioration, massive resource consumption and low recycling rate, have become barriers to the sustainable development of the Chinese economy. In the course of economic and social development, China is faced with a series of fight-at-two-fronts tasks, including how to achieve rapid economic growth whilst stepping up social development during the coordinated development of economy and society; how to accelerate technological progress and industrial progress whilst increasing social employment; how to maintain great development momentum in eastern China whilst promoting common development of eastern, central and western China; how to advance urbanization whilst helping the countryside develop in every aspect; how to pay attention to justice and narrow gaps whilst maintaining vitality and improving efficiency; how to attract more investment whilst improving investment structure; how to trade market for technology whilst strengthening independent technological innovation; how to further reform whilst maintaining social stability; and how to promote market competition whilst caring for the working conditions and life of the needy. To address all these challenges and issues, we cannot disregard any of them but strive to achieve sustainable, healthy economic and social development by taking into account all factors.

Since the 18th CPC National Congress, the CPC Central Committee with Xi Jinping at the core have deliberated over and studied these issues. Their conclusion is that after four decades of rapid development, China now faces an economic new normal never seen before. Now that one-sided pursuit of GDP growth no longer works, they have set forth the philosophy of people-centered development and the new concepts of innovative, coordinated, green, open and shared development consistent with the philosophy. At the Belt and Road Forum for International Cooperation, after expounding that the Belt and Road is a road for peace, a road of prosperity, a road of opening up, a road of innovation and a road connecting civilizations, President Xi Jinping also articulates, "China has reached a new starting point in its development endeavors. Guided by the vision of innovative, coordinated, green, open and inclusive development, we will adapt to and steer the new normal of economic development and seize opportunities it presents. We will actively promote supply-side structural reform to achieve sustainable development, inject strong impetus into the Belt and Road Initiative and create new opportunities for global development." [13]

It is evident that the peaceful rise today pays more attention to high-quality growth, to coordinated, shared development of all parties, and to green, low-carbon development. The core concept through the peaceful rise strategy is the people-centered concept. The CPC Central Committee stresses that improving people's well-being and promoting individuals' well-rounded development should be made the starting point and ultimate goal of development. All these important thoughts present the new prospect of China's path of peaceful rise in the new round of economic globalization.

Thirdly, the new prospect of China's peaceful rise is new in that China has started from its historic position in the new era and pushed forth reform and opening up in an all-round way, raising the Chinese people's productivity to an unprecedented new height in the forefront of the world by following the new path of peaceful rise.

---

[13] *People's Daily*, May 15, 2017.

This is yet another new characteristic of China's path of peaceful rise amidst the new round of economic growth. In the important speech at the World Economic Forum in Davos, President Xi Jinping says when expounding China's path, "China has become the world's second largest economy thanks to 38 years of reform and opening up. A right path leads to a bright future. China has come this far because the Chinese people have, under the leadership of the Communist Party of China, blazed a development path that suits China's actual conditions."[14] He stresses that China's path of development is a path based on China's realities, a path that puts people's interests first, a path of pursuing reform and innovation, and a path of pursuing common development through opening-up. That is, China has in the past years succeeded in embarking on a development path that suits itself by drawing on both the wisdom of its civilization and the practices of other countries in both East and West. In exploring this path, China refuses to stay insensitive to the changing times or to blindly follow in others' footsteps. In other words, China follows a people-oriented development philosophy and is committed to bettering the lives of its people. Development is of the people, by the people and for the people. China pursues the goal of common prosperity. We have taken major steps to alleviate poverty and lifted over 700 million people out of poverty, and good progress is being made in our efforts to finish building a society of initial prosperity in all respects. To put it in another way, China has tackled difficulties and met challenges on its way forward through reform. China has demonstrated its courage to take on difficult issues, navigate treacherous rapids and remove institutional hurdles standing in the way of development. These efforts have enabled us to unleash productivity and social vitality. Building on progress of 30-odd years of reform, we have introduced more than 1,200 reform measures

---

[14] *People's Daily*, January 18, 2017.

over the past four years, injecting powerful impetus into China's development.

Here I would like to say, we have always remembered affectionately a passage in Mao's report to the 7th CPC National Congress, "In the last analysis, the impact, good or bad, great or small, of the policy and the practice of any Chinese political party upon the people depends on whether and how much it helps to develop their productive forces, and on whether it fetters or liberates these forces."[15] Today there is a task throughout the entire primary stage of socialism, which is to increase the Chinese people's productivity and improve its quality in a sustained, efficient way. The new era which socialism with Chinese characteristics has entered is a critical period for the completion of all strategic tasks of the primary stage of socialism. It happens in this period that two unprecedented events take place – first, the integration of the new era and the new round of economic globalization, and second, the integration of industrialization and modernization with informatization and the new revolution of science and technology. The Chinese people's modern productivity with science and technology, the primary productive force, is injecting vigor to the new era. This is also a new opportunity for China's peaceful rise. Only by seizing the opportunity can the Chinese people's productivity be raised to a new height and put China in the world forefront in the mid-21st century.

Fourthly, the new prospect of China's peaceful rise is also new in that China offers a brand-new option and provides necessary aid to those countries and nations in the world which hope to accelerate development and maintain independence, promoting the common peaceful development of all countries, particularly developing countries, by pursuing the new path of peaceful rise.

---

[15] Mao Zedong: "On Coalition Government," *Selected Works of Mao Tse-Tung*, Vol. III, Foreign Languages Press, 1965, p. 251.

The Communist Party of China is a party which seeks happiness for the Chinese people and fights for the cause of human progress. As President Xi Jinping says at the CPC in Dialogue with World Parties High-level Meeting, the CPC strives for the well-being of the Chinese people, rejuvenation of the Chinese nation as well as peace and development of mankind. Taking good care of China's internal matters is part of China's contribution to building a community with a shared future for mankind. The CPC will create opportunities for the world through China's development and explore the law of social development for humanity and share it with other countries. Meanwhile, he also stresses, we will neither import foreign models of development nor export the Chinese model. We will not ask other countries to copy the Chinese practice.

At the Belt and Road Forum for International Cooperation, President Xi Jinping says, China will enhance friendship and cooperation with all countries involved in the Belt and Road Initiative on the basis of the Five Principles of Peaceful Co-existence. In pursuing the Belt and Road Initiative, we will not resort to outdated geopolitical manoeuvring. What we hope to achieve is a new model of win-win cooperation. We do not intend to form a small group detrimental to stability, what we hope to create is a big family of harmonious co-existence. China is ready to share practices of development with other countries, but does not intend to interfere in other countries' internal affairs, export our own social system and model of development, or impose our own will on others. Since the launch of the Belt and Road Initiative, China has reached practical cooperation agreements with many countries. These agreements cover not only projects of hardware connectivity, like transport, infrastructure and energy, but also software connectivity, involving telecommunications, customs and quarantine inspection. The agreements also include plans and projects for cooperation in economy and trade, industry, e-commerce, marine and green economy. China will endeavor to build a win-win busi-

August 8, 2017. On a field trip to Gansu Province

ness partnership with other countries participating in the Belt and Road Initiative, enhance trade and investment facilitation with them, and build a Belt and Road free trade network. These efforts are designed to promote growth both in our respective regions and globally.

China will scale up financing support for the Belt and Road Initiative by contributing an additional RMB100 billion to the Silk Road Fund, and will encourage financial institutions to conduct overseas RMB fund business to an estimated value of about RMB300 billion. The China Development Bank and the Export-Import Bank of China will set up special lending schemes respectively worth RMB250 billion equivalent and RMB130 billion equivalent to support Belt and Road cooperation on infrastructure, industrial capacity and financing. We will also work with the Asian Infrastructure Investment Bank (AIIB), the BRICS New Development Bank, the World Bank and other multilateral development institutions to support Belt and Road related projects. We will work with other parties concerned to jointly formulate guidelines for financing

Belt and Road related development projects. We will provide emergency food aid worth RMB 2 billion to developing countries along the Belt and Road and make an additional contribution of US$1 billion to the Assistance Fund for South-South Cooperation. China will launch 100 "happy home" projects, 100 poverty alleviation projects and 100 health care and rehabilitation projects in countries along the Belt and Road. China will provide relevant international organizations with US$1 billion to implement cooperation projects that will benefit the countries along the Belt and Road. That China actively advances mutually beneficial win-win construction of the Belt and Road in collaboration with the Belt and Road countries can be said an important measure to better facilitate the common peaceful rise of developing countries.

All this has convincingly proven that the Communist Party of China has made it its own mission to make new greater contributions to humankind and thus demonstrated that the Chinese people are willing to work with peoples of other countries to build the global community of shared future and fulfil their common sincere wishes for peaceful rise under the themes of peace and development and in the context of the multi-polar world pattern. These important thoughts also visualize the new prospect of China's path of peaceful rise in the new round of economic globalization.

Concluding Words: Twenty-five Points of Deliberation

Before finishing the manuscript, I would like to document my train of thought on economic globalization and China's peaceful rise through the years since the late 1980s.

My thinking can be summed up in one sentence – in the historical context underscoring peace and development, in a process connected with rather than detached from economic globalization, China has been independently building socialism with Chinese characteristics and striving to achieve its peaceful rise.

This conclusion can be elaborated in the following twenty-five points:

First, as I see it, the major changes to the internal and international imperatives are the determinant. The major changes in China refer to the reform and opening up policies the Communist Party of China decided to implement in 1978. The major changes in the world refer to the dawn of a new era, roughly after the end of the Vietnam War and the Soviet War in Afghanistan; this period of time can be characterized by the launch of the 3rd round of economic globalization, wherein peace and development are the backdrop in the world.

Second, associated with these major changes is China's new awakening, which is essentially about "catching up with the times and ushering in a new era" – embodied in reform and opening up geared toward economic globalization and modernization as well as the patriotism of the new era. Love of the country has always been a source of inspiration for socialism with Chinese characteristics.

Third, an important proposition brought by the major changes and new awakening is "the strategic path of China's peaceful rise." And the path, as I put it, is to build socialism with Chinese characteristics independently and through a process that is connected with rather than detached from economic globalization.

Fourth, the path of peaceful rise creates the Chinese way, the Chinese dream and the Chinese heart. I need to stress that the course of peaceful rise refers specifically to the period of about 70 years, known as the primary stage of socialism, from the start of reform and opening up in the late 1970s, through the stages of "adequate food and clothing," "preliminary moderate prosperity" and "all-round prosperity," to the accomplishment of full modernization in the mid-21st century. What extends throughout the much longer historical period of socialism in China, on the other hand, is development, or peaceful development, from beginning to end.

Fifth, the term "peaceful rise" has another connotation – it is a response to certain theories in the world community. The word "peaceful" responds to the "China threat" theory and the word "rise" to "the collapse of China" theory.

Sixth, I have several times stated that in the present world, China is only one of many developing countries that are all striving to achieve peaceful rise with their respective characteristics. The coming decade will be a critical period for a joint peaceful rise of developing countries, while the developed countries are trying to achieve further development.

Seventh, duality – the inherent trait of everything in the world – means that there are always two possibilities, positive and negative, success and failure. In my opinion, this is an important way of thinking that prepares people psychologically – something I have stressed repeatedly when I discuss the need to "grasp the overall situation with a sober mind."

Eighth, on the basis of the "major changes," "new awakening" and "duality," I emphasized "the common interests worldwide and communities of shared interests at different levels with different contents" regarding international relations whilst proposing the concept of "peaceful rise." I believe that this should be an important long-term concept while China builds inter-state relations in the new era. This concept captured the attention of and won favor with US strategists Henry Kissinger and Zbigniew Brzezinski. The 21st Century Council, an international think tank, has decided to adopt it as its guiding idea.

Ninth, as to the current international situation, I believe that China, the United States and Russia are forming "a great triangle" that differs from the axis of the Cold War era. Though there are disparities in strength between them, the trend is there. I call it "the new triangle."

Tenth, as to China's current surrounding environment, things are very different along the north and south borderlines. I have termed the situation "the two lines."

Eleventh, the profound impacts of the world financial crisis are not completely resolved. There remain factors of uncertainty in the course of world economic recovery. Non-traditional security issues such as climate, resources, crops and finance are becoming prominent. The issue of global governance is crying out for resolution.

Twelfth, various challenges still exist, including serious turmoil, geopolitical conflicts, the specters of terrorism, populism, and traditional war. People should neither be over-fearful about them, nor disregard them.

Thirteenth, the international financial crisis and the on-going new revolution of science and technology have caused major changes to patterns of work worldwide. The new revolution in science, technology and industry, with intelligent and Internet technologies at the core, is becoming increasingly prominent.

Fourteenth, the modes of economic growth of major powers will undergo significant change, which will lead to a further reshuffle of their respective status.

Fifteenth, in the final analysis, the world's major powers will move in three directions: first, sticking to the Cold War mentality; second, engaging in local conflict; and third, seeking common development and mutual benefit. We are opposed to the first two approaches, which lead us nowhere, but we do not fear them. China has dealt with them successfully in the past. But our preference is for the third. That is, in the context of economic globalization, on the basis of building its own strengths, China will follow the development path of peaceful rise, search for common interests with all related countries and regions in an all-round manner, and build communities of shared interests at different levels and with different aims. By "all-round," we mean that we seek to work with the United States, with Europe, with other Asian countries – particularly neighboring countries – with Africa, and with Latin America. Our approach is by no means exclusive.

Sixteenth, as to the latest developments: On the one hand, Western developed countries, represented first and foremost by the United States, are creating an anti-globalization trend in ideology and politics. On the other hand, the peaceful rise of emerging countries is thriving. The magnificent Belt and Road initiative launched by China, in particular, is unfolding; it marks a historical turning point. After four decades, the third round of economic globalization is coming to an end. After a rather long transitional period, the world will welcome in a new stage – the fourth round of economic globalization.

Seventeenth, I also believe that besides other attributes, the fourth round of economic globalization is likely to have two major features – one, a general trend under which emerging economies will surpass developed economies in total economic aggregate will continue; and two, as the Belt and Road initiative unfolds and sustained efforts are made, maritime economic globalization spanning the Atlantic and the Pacific, formed over hundreds of years, will evolve into maritime and continental economic globalization characterized by offshore-inland connectivity.

Eighteenth, however international relationships shift, humanity will, for a long period to come, remain in the historical stage of sovereign states.

Nineteenth, both China and the world are currently faced with a situation characterized by interlinked opportunities and challenges, with more opportunities than challenges. As the global power balance shifts, China is in an advantageous position. We have confidence in China's peaceful rise in the second decade of the 21st century.

Twentieth, the major changes, new awakening, and various shifts have brought about ideological clashes both at home and abroad. I call this the worldwide coexistence of "different schools" from the late 20th century to the early 21st century.

Twenty-first, I believe that the solemn resolve of the Communist Party of China to achieve its lofty missions of the rejuvenation of the Chinese nation and the rejuvenation of the Chinese civilization in the mid-21st century is in accord with rather than in opposition to economic globalization and other contemporary schools of thinking

Twenty-second, I also hold that the cornerstone and indication of China's rejuvenation is its impressive economic growth.

Apart from economic growth, China will also achieve great leaps forward in national defense, cultural awareness, and governance. Together these four forces make up what the Chinese often refer to as material and cultural civilization, and are of extraordinary significance to China's